"He who believes in Me, as the Scripture has said, out of his heart will flow rivers of living water" – John 7:38

"For I know the plans I have for you", declares the Lord, "Plans to prosper you and not harm you, plans to give you hope and a future"–Jeremiah 29:11

Transformation of the Heart:
A Renewed Life

Susana J. Bertuna, Ph.D.

WESTBOW
PRESS®
A DIVISION OF THOMAS NELSON
& ZONDERVAN

This book is a work of non-fiction. Unless otherwise noted, the author and the publisher make no explicit guarantees as to the accuracy of the information contained in this book and in some cases, names of people and places have been altered to protect their privacy.

WestBow Press books may be ordered through booksellers or by contacting:

WestBow Press
A Division of Thomas Nelson & Zondervan
1663 Liberty Drive
Bloomington, IN 47403
www.westbowpress.com
1 (866) 928-1240

Scripture taken from the New King James Version®. Copyright © 1982 by Thomas Nelson. Used by permission. All rights reserved.

ISBN: 978-1-9736-1146-2 (sc)
ISBN: 978-1-9736-1145-5 (e)

Library of Congress Cataloging-in-Publication Data
Bertuna, Susana
Registration Number
TXu 2-063-626

Print information available on the last page.

WestBow Press rev. date: 02/08/2018

Dedication

For my papá Salvatore, your spirit lives on
For my twins Eliana Gabriela and Dario Elias
Miracles and gifts from God
I love you more…
1111

Tribute

Life is a beautiful gift, a journey that accumulates still moments and archives memories. A life in which we can dance whimsically and paint with strokes of colors. This book is a tribute to a young life taken from us too soon – Jacob Dylan Rivera who went home to be with the Lord on November 18, 2017. In memory of his short life, but one that touched so many lives while doing God's work, Jacob's light and legacy will live on.

Part of the proceeds from the sale of this book will be donated to:
CCS Memorial Fund – In memory of Jacob Dylan Rivera - (3/10/1999 -11/18/2017)

https://www.youcaring.com/calvarychristianschool-1037199

This was Jacob's life verse –

"Bless those who persecute you; bless and do not curse. Rejoice with those that rejoice, and weep with those who weep." - Romans 12:14-15

"Therefore if the Son makes you free, you shall be free indeed" – John 8:36

Acknowledgements

To my Lord and Savior, Jesus Christ for the gift of eternal life. To my Redeemer and Maker, is all the Glory. You commissioned each one of us for a purpose as we all have a testimony, and a Jesus story to tell – this is mine. To my husband Elias, thank you for the beautiful family we have. To my teenage twins, Eliana and Dario, thank you for your unconditional love. You sustain my motivation, drive, and inspiration. I love you with all my heart for how special each one of you are in my life's journey. To my mamá Josephine, all present family members, and to family members that once shared our family table too - Isabel, Gianni, Sibel, and Dino: may God always light your paths, protect your hearts, and bless you immensely. To my Fabian, thank you for your beautiful heart, I can tell already that God resides in it. To Ismael, thank you - I did find purpose and truth; it was simply waiting for me - "somewhere out there…"

To those that have passed on - papá Salvatore, tio Pepe, Fita, Nonna, Nonno, tia Graciana, tio Salvador, and my sweet Pebbles- we will see each other again, in heaven. To the town of Vizzini, in Sicily, Italy, through the winding hills where no matter how you enter the town, a very distinct and majestic tree seen from far welcomes you. Once you see that tall tree, Vizzini awaits. This is where all my ancestors were born and many returned to be buried there. They were bold and courageous to leave their beloved town of Vizzini in search of new opportunities amongst the many long and far away roads in the world. You all have impacted many generations in our family tree.

To my beloved Argentina, country and land where I was born, where my precious childhood took place in Barrio San Jose - I extend with deep gratitude to my far away family, and friends a heartfelt thank you for always keeping my childhood memories alive. Thank you for reminding me to always be proud of my roots, and never forget where I came from.

To the amazing and courageous fourteen men who were interviewed, thank you for your vulnerability, trust and amazing love for God. Your street smarts and emotional intelligence was your guide to choose repentance, and humbleness for a renewed life. You tapped into the extraordinary, and the highest IQ of all - GOD. You all gave me a valuable gift to carry on in my life; you let me into your past, allowed me to meet you in your present, and shared your hope of a future. You have transformed your hearts, and you taught me that only through the mercy and grace from God it was possible.

You taught me that it is not religion, but it is all about a relationship with our Lord and Savior. You exercised free will and choose Him to dwell in your heart. Rewarded with a transformed and ready heart you tell others of Him, and that is how we met. You radiate inner peace, joy, freedom, and are a blessing to others. You have been chosen to be light in this world. God is Good! Thank you all for being warriors of love and goodness.

To my spiritual mentors Pastor Al Scavone and Dorla Perry, thank you for always guiding me through His word and your prayers. Dr. Dustin Berna, thank you for seeing the writer in me. Dr. Ralph Hogges thank you for inspiring me to leave a legacy through books for the generations to come. Dr. Gwendolyn Smith, thank you for your sincere and beautiful friendship. To Kim Dolcimascolo, thank you for your unwavering mentorship and for being an amazing human being. Indeed, everything is possible when you choose to contribute and be of service to others, and what you are rewarded with is an extraordinary life. To Terry Dorsey, thank you for your support and believing in me. I did promise to write for the voiceless one day, and with this book I fulfill that promise. My strength is being a free spirit, and only the Lord gives me that strength and vitality in life.

Contents

Chapter 1: Introduction 1

    Definitions and Terms 2

    Summary 4

Chapter 2: Purpose of the Study 5

    Conceptual Framework 5

    Grounded Theory Methodology 5

    Participants 7

    Data Collection 8

    Data Analysis 9

    Research Methodology 11

    Reliability 13

    Validity 13

    Researcher Biases 14

    Ethical Considerations 15

    Summary 15

Chapter 3: Data Analysis and Results 17

    Research Questions 17

Chapter 4: Thematic Analysis 1 21

Chapter 5: Thematic Analysis 2 29

Chapter 6: Thematic Analysis 3 37

Chapter 7: Thematic Analysis 4 45

Chapter 8: Findings and Emerging Themes **55**

Chapter 9: The Grounded Theory HOPE© **57**

Strengths and Limitations of the Study 58

Implications for the field of Conflict Analysis and Resolution 59

Chapter 10: Proposal of MAPCID© Model **61**

Reflections of the Author 63

Concluding Comments and Thoughts 64

References 67

List of Tables

Table 1: Participants' Socio-Demographics Profiles...19

Table 2: The Childhood Life Experiences of the Former Gang Members Prior to Their Involvement with Their Respective Gangs 22

Table 3: How Former Gang Members Perceive Social Morality and the Role of Religion across Different Life Stages- During Their Affiliation with the Gang.................29

Table 4: How Former Gang Members Perceive Social Morality and the Role of Religion across Different Life Stages – After Their Affiliation with the Gang..................37

Table 5: The Life-Changing Events that Made Former Gang Members Leave their Gang Affiliations...46

List of Figures

Figure 1: Thematic analysis – three basic stages (Attride-Stirling, 2001) 12

Figure 2: Thematic Networks (Attride-Stirling, 2001) 13

Figure 3: Participants' socio-demographic profiles: Age.................................... 20

Figure 4: Participants' socio-demographic profiles: Ethinicity............................ 20

Figure 5: Participants' socio-demographic profiles: Education level........................ 20

Figure 6: Graph representation of Table 2 – Theme 1...................................... 22

Figure 7: Graph representation of Table 3 – Theme 2...................................... 30

Figure 8: Graph representation of Table 4 – Theme 3...................................... 38

Figure 9: Graph representation of Table 5 – Theme 4...................................... 46

Figure 10: Thematic categories summary – findings and emerging themes 54

Figure 11: Model of emergence of themes 56

Figure 12: Model for Grounded Theory—HOPE©: Holistic Outreach Program for Exit....... 58

Figure 13: MAPCID©: Model for the Analysis of Potential Conflict in Development
(Smith, Michaud, Bertuna-Reynoso, & Struss, 2014) 61

— CHAPTER 1 —
Introduction

This literature review found some evidence that religious and faith-based programming can have some success in disengaging persons from gang membership. The review found that gang membership is on the rise in the South and all over the U.S. (Howell, 2010; Rivera, 2010; Tortoroli, 2011; Zdun, 2008). The review also found that the research into why youth join gangs is only at the moment approaching a consensus. A major theme that has emerged in the gang formation research is that the gang becomes an alternative family providing a sense of belonging to youth who have accumulated a number of risk factors relating to disintegrated family life (Alleyne & Wood, 2010; Decker & Pyrooz, 2011; Dnes & Garoupa, 2010; Fleisher, 2009; Grekul & LaBoucane-Benson, 2008; Hottman, 2009; Katz & Fox, 2010; King & Furrow, 2004; White, 2009). Further, the review found that though police and the criminal justice system continue to espouse a suppression approach to gang membership, focusing on crime and, with mixed results, social and school-based programming have emerged which focus on all the risk factors cited for membership and address those factors one by one (Eghighan & Kirby, 2006). Thus, programs that focus on individual, family, community, and social and school or institutionalized reasons for gang membership cumulatively tend to have the most success in preventing gang membership.

The review found that with the rise of immigrant youth joining gangs, in particularly Latinos, cultural values have been brought into the intervention models, some with a focus on spirituality. Research has established that religious values or spirituality can help youth avoid many of the pitfalls of adolescence in terms of social or mental problems, forming the basis of interventions focused on religion (Arthur, 2009; Bangerter, 2010; Bermudez, 2008; Brenneman, 2009; Brenneman, 2010; Buxant & Saroglou, 2008; Byassee, 2007; Cruz, 2006; Duffin, 2011; Gardner, 2011; Haynes, 2012; Hoke, 2012; Johnson, 2011; Riley, 2006; Sun, 2011; Van Dyke, 2006). With regard to gang exit or leaving gangs, a number of programs have been developed based on observations of gang membership by several theoretical models. This has led to gang exit programs which focus on social as well as religious values, offering tattoo removal as a strategy to enable a change of identity, often combined with meeting housing and other needs as well as spiritual needs in transitioning out of gangs. The primary model for this type of gang exit model is that, insofar as the gang itself had become an alternative community to compensate gang members for weak families, so the creation of another alternative community and attracting gang members from one to another would be successful. Religion and faith-based communities emerged to offer such an alternative community by which a gang member could trade one form of masculinity for another in transforming oneself out of the group. Because of the social and emotional nature of this transformation involved in finding a new sense of belonging, the symbolic value of tattoo removal and the role that spirituality can play have emerged as key program elements.

The review also found a few case studies of best practice programs making use of religion in various ways to dislodge gang members from gangs (Calhoun, 2012; Flores, 2010; Tyler, 2012). In one case study, the Catholic method for prevention of gang membership was not found to be as effective as the Pentecostal approach, using tattoo removal and testimony, as well as other religious services, all of which provided emotional platforms in the context of which a former gang member could transform from one type of person into another. Overall, while no case study emerged of a faith-based gang exit program in Florida, the review found that faith-based programs, especially if modeled on two of the most studied programs in California, could be effective in expediting gang exit for gang members.

Definitions and Terms

Gang: a faction of individuals sharing similar interest and motivation to control communal territories through engagement in violent behaviors and other illegal acts purposely to harass and perpetuate fear in the community (Billitteri, 2010). Gang is an informal social structure with a defined leadership and organization arrangement and is organized to collectively perform violence (Duffin, 2011; Gardner, 2011). As the definition suggests, a gang denotes a criminal organization mostly organized and led by criminals who denounce moral actions by engaging in violent behaviors that deter the safety of citizens. The early definition of gang states,

> an interstitial group originally formed spontaneous, and then integrated through conflict. It is characterized by the following types of behavior: meeting face-to-face, milling, movement through space as a unit, conflict, and planning. The result of this collective behavior is the development of tradition, unreflective internal structure, esprit de corps, solidarity, morale, group awareness, and attachment to a local territory. (Thrasher, 1927, p. 57)

Former gang member: an individual or person who has been rehabilitated or departed from gang affiliation through the process of a moral and social integration program (Brenneman, 2009, 2010).

Gang exit: a process of departure of a gang member to known gang characteristics, behaviors, crimes, and weakness of involvement in any gang related activities. Studies concerning gang exit implicate offending and victimization, pro social relationship, and collateral consequences against the neighborhood and family as factors causing the departure of an individual to gang affiliation (Duffin, 2011; Gardner, 2011).

Gang unit: a measure used to determine the capacity of a group or groups to provide danger within the neighborhood environment (Kelly, 2010). Gang unit identifies and assesses the risk factors associated with the characteristics and behaviors of the gang as well as the affiliated members (Billitteri, 2010).

Gang member: an individual who chooses to reject mainstreamed value systems and lives in violence along with their co-members. Gang member has been commonly referred as gangster in the U.S. and mobster in the United Kingdom. Since gang member has a high tolerance of violence and performs violent behaviors, it is most likely that a gang member has been arrested or has been through the criminal justice system.

Gang membership/affiliation: gang is known for the establishment of distinctive physical characteristics, type of crime engagement, and criminal behaviors which indicate membership and/or affiliation. Seeking gang membership, therefore, requires practicing set and identified characteristics such as the wearing of clothing and accessory identifiers and engaging in either individual or collective violent acts (Kelly, 2010).

Transformation: within the framework of gang formation, social transformation happens when challenging events confront the value system of a gang member (Koffman, Ray, Berg, Covington, Albarran, & Vasquez, 2009).

Transcendence: a spiritual term used to refer to the secular consciousness of an individual engaged with immoral acts and behaviors (Flores, 2010; Tyler, 2012).

Rehabilitation program: these are strategies and activities that restore an individual's deviant behaviors to the mainstreamed and acceptable norms and behaviors (Billitteri, 2010).

Transnational gang: a criminal organization organized to operate serious transnational criminal activities such as sex and drug trafficking, kidnapping, assassination, human and goods smuggling, immigration offenses, and extortion among others (Krohn, Ward, Thornberry, Lizotte, & Chu, 2011).

While there has been no consensus or standard definition for to the term *gang*, the socio-political view associates gang to community nuance, which can affect achievement of peace and development of the individual, the families, and communities (Baier & Wright, 2001). Gang has been historically associated to crimes and the criminal behaviors of mostly delinquents struggling for social acceptance (Yearwood & Hayes, 2000). Years of research explored the value of religion and spirituality in the deterrence of criminal behaviors particularly among these delinquents (Akers, 2010; Johnson, 1987a, 1987b; Jones, 2006; Richards, 1916). Spiritual practice generates multiple benefits to individuals especially in establishing positive connection with others as well as disposition with the inner self (Kerley, Matthews, & Blanchard, 2005). This made the practice of religion more relevant for programs for incarceration facilities (Grobsmith, 1994; Johnson, 2004; Smith, 1995).

The association of gang membership and religion emerged as a profound concept in the social transformation and rehabilitation of incarcerated and former gang members (Arthur, 2009; Bangerter, 2010). Studies postulating the efficacy of the use of religion in the disengagement of incarcerated gang members recommend in-depth investigation concerning a faith-based approach in order to subsequently deter the escalating number of street crimes involving gang members (Calhoun, 2012; Flores, 2010; Tyler, 2012). This grounded study explores the transformational changes of individuals involved in gang membership.

Summary

Research concludes that there is a positive link from religion and religious practices to an individual's commitment to positive morality (Johnson, 2004). Similarly, the element of religion plays a significant factor in persuading an individual to disengage from the affiliated gang. As such, several governmental incarceration programs tapped into organized religious groups to provide and guide incarcerated individuals in religiosity, which can be used to support the process of their social transformation. However, while religion has been linked positively to the morality and social transformation of an individual, there is a dearth of research that explains the role of religion in the lives of an individual affiliated with organized gang membership. This grounded theory research explored the transformational changes of individuals involved in gang membership by examining the lives of former gang members who are now affiliated with organized religious groups in Florida.

— CHAPTER 2 —
Purpose of the Study

The purpose of this qualitative grounded theory research was to develop a theory concerning the application of faith-based approach to rehabilitation programs based on the experiences and perceptions of males who were former members of community gangs from Latin America, Central America, and the United States living in the United States. The study sought to understand the social dynamic of religion as it relates to gang membership by determining the contribution of faith-based rehabilitation programs to the lives of former male gang members from families in Florida, United States. The study was designed to recruit and invite the former gang members who are now religiously affiliated with Christianity in Florida to participate in a semi-structured face-to-face interview. By examining the former gang members' lived experiences, perceptions of reality, and transformational change, the realm of religiosity in light of the social dimension of the individual involved in criminal acts were further contemplated.

Conceptual Framework

The conceptual idea of this research was that religion and the views of social morality of the individual shape his decision to transform from a gang affiliated member to become a member of a moral and religious group that denounces criminal acts. For this study, the main problem was to understand (via the participants) if religion and gang membership can be described in discrete terms that can be replicated and operationalized in an approach that can be used for the rehabilitation program specifically for male gang affiliated members in the United States.

Grounded Theory Methodology

A grounded theory research design was used to support the generation of a theory that is most appropriate for the application of a faith-based approach to rehabilitation programs of male gang members living in the United States. As used in this study, the grounded theory takes a qualitative research stance that generates probable conclusion of the phenomenon through the empirical evidences as experienced by an individual (Glaser, 1978). A qualitative research uses the *interpretivist* perspective, rather than a *positivist* view as in quantitative research. Interpretivist and positivist approaches differ by the types of questions asked regarding the data and the types of conclusions drawn by the researcher (Lin, 1998). For instance, the interpretivist perspective may ask *how* and *what* questions that understand a phenomenon while the positivist perspective may ask a defined question answerable by either one or two answers. The qualitative research approach is appropriate when the intention of the researcher is to evaluate details pertaining to preferences, motivations, and actions not easily made numeric. A positivist perspective identifies the details with propositions tested or identified in other cases, whereas an interpretivist view combines those details into systems of belief whose manifestations are specific to a case (Lin, 1998). As a positivist, a researcher works to interpret general patterns, but an interpretivist researcher works to explain how the general pattern applies in practice.

According to Creswell (2005), qualitative research is appropriate to use when the intention of the researcher is to garner an understanding of a paradigm in which little is known about the problem or variables prior to the study. In this context, qualitative research is appropriate to use in describing the experiences or feelings of a small number of subjects who provide their own explanations in a given setting. As opposed to quantitative research, qualitative research uses the small number of subjects who have relative experience of the studied phenomenon.

The researcher of a qualitative study is "not necessarily detached from the research but may actually be involved in the contextual situation of the participant" (Simon & Francis, 2001, p. 40) because it utilizes a more personal approach with the participant during the process. For instance, a qualitative researcher connects his or her experiences to understand the behavior of each of the participants of the study. Qualitative research is exploratory, which incorporates the researchers' experiences to provide a better understanding of the phenomena. With a pragmatic approach, the researcher can be open to discovering applicable variables or desirable themes which may enable appropriate examination of the individual's experiences.

According to Denzin and Lincoln (2005), qualitative research is multi-method in focus, involving an interpretive, naturalist approach to its subject matter. It also involves a collection of empirical materials gathered by the researcher through interviews and observations and documented in case studies, which include personal experiences and introspective reflections. Bogdan and Biklen (2006) described qualitative research as understanding how people make and live their lives. Qualitative research allows researchers to investigate the interpretations and meanings of the participants' actual settings (Seidman, 2006).

Research in qualitative methodology includes a variety of types such as biography, grounded theory, ethnography, case study, and phenomenology. These types have commonalities in their designs including: a) focusing on a single individual; b) constructing a study from stories and epiphanies of special events and situating them within a broader context; and c) evoking the presence of the narrator in the study (Merriam as cited in Flick et al., 2007). For this particular study, grounded theory was the most appropriate because the method can formulate a premise based on conceptual ideas (Glaser & Strauss, 1967).

Grounded theory was developed by Barney Glaser and Anselm Strauss (1967) after jointly undertaking a health research project (Glaser, 1965). While both of them can be credited as fathers of the grounded theory methodology, researchers who used either of their work must note that they came from two different schools of thought. Glaser (1992) used the induction method of generating research conclusions while Strauss (1987) was a pragmatist who believed that philosophical issues could be addressed by examining the practical uses or successes behind the issue. Glaser was educated at a Columbia University in New York while Strauss came from the University of Chicago (Glaser & Strauss, 1967). The differences in the authors' views resulted in two schools of thought for grounded theory, the Glaserian School and the Straussian School (Stern, 1994). The research method and design for this study employed the Glaserian method, which takes the position that the researcher approaches the study with a blank canvas; hence, the researcher leads with the belief that theory should manifest. Grounded theory supports developing innovative theory encompassing interconnected thoughts, perceptions, and beliefs rather than investigating existing theories. A study led by grounded theory does not search for achievement of statistical generalizability but instead seeks to enlighten and often times foretell phenomena based on experiential data.

Grounded theory is a systematic approach to the collection, coding, and analysis of data to resolve concerns and understand how issues would be dealt with. Glaserian grounded theory uses the inductive method of reasoning that based its generalization on what the people know concerning the phenomenon (Glaser, 1992). Grounded theory is a way to address and conceptualize the problem based on what and how these problems came to be in the light of the experiences of those individuals who possess the knowledge and experience concerning the phenomenon (Glaser, 1978). In this case, the approach was the generation of appropriate theory by understanding faith-based approaches to rehabilitation programs of male gang members living in the USA. Perceptions of social morality and religion have been theoretically cited as elements of the individual life transformation. However, none from the reviewed studies has further examined the use and contribution of these elements in the exploration of the faith-based approach to rehabilitation programs of male gang members. By approaching the problem with no consistent, standardized set faith-based approach for male gang member rehabilitation program through grounded theory, it is possible to formulate (retrospectively) a theory to fit and support the data gathered in interviews.

Participants

Former gang members are those individual who have been rehabilitated from gang affiliation through the process of integrating the moral acts and religion as a fundamental way of life guiding their social behavior. While this description may be subjective, the objective attributes of the former gang members who may qualify in the present study were: a) male adults between the ages of 21 to 60 years, b) former gang members who attended faith-based programs within churches, and c) able to sustain the life transformation as a result of attending faith-based rehabilitation programs.

Qualitative research normally involves small sample sizes of participants, as opposed to quantitative research which normally relies on larger sample sizes. Creswell (2005) recommended that the size of a qualitative sample should range from 1-25 participants, and Polkinghorne (2005) suggested that qualitative research include sample sizes of 5 to 25 participants. Patton (2002) stated that there are no specific rules for sample size, suggesting that "Sample size depends on what you want to know, the purpose of the inquiry, what's at stake, what will be useful, what will have credibility, and what can be done with available time and resources" (p. 244). The qualitative study can accommodate sample sizes from 5 to 25 or more participants; thus, the sample size for the present study was largely up to the researcher. Most qualitative studies tend to use between 10 and 20 participants. For this study, the purposive sample of 14 participants was taken from the list of the church administrators of faith-based programs. The number of participants was consistent with the required number for a sample that can offer themes for analysis. The target sample of 14 participants was an effective choice as it is only permitted the downsizing of the participants at a lower level when saturation of data is realized at the early stage of data collection.

Data Collection

Many factors were involved in the consideration of appropriate research methods for data collection and instrumentation. The factors included the need for data from subject matter experts, access to a representative population, and varied perspectives from diverse participants.

Creswell (2009) identified observations, interviews, documents, and audio-visual materials as forms of data collection. The use of unstructured observational data in different venues as a participant observer or non-participant observer is not available and precludes the opportunity to take field notes or to record data to inform the research. The most appropriate and available data collection method to achieve data validity and reliability in the target population frame was the semi-structured interview (Bryant & Charmaz, 2007).

The face-to-face interview using semi-structured questions provided the most appropriate instrument to understand the central phenomenon of a faith-based approach to rehabilitation of former gang affiliated members because most of the emphasis is on the role of the researcher to elicit and represent an interpretive relationship of the phenomenon (Hiller & DiLuzio, 2004). Face-to-face interviews in qualitative research have advantages and disadvantages (Rubin & Rubin, 1995). The advantages include direct contact by the researcher with the research participants, a commonly accepted protocol for valid qualitative research, the costs associated with data collection involving recording of interviews and transcription of results, and the generation of a large volume of research data from the transcribed interviews (Creswell, 2009). The disadvantages include time to collect data, less access to research participants, and difficulty in replication of the research.

Using the purposive sampling process of reaching 14 participants described in an earlier subsection helped ensure that sample participants were credible as representatives of the former gang affiliated members. The face-to-face interview as well ensured that interviews of the participants were recorded and transcribed. The transcription of the interview was sent via email to the respective participants for peer-checking and validation. The data collection procedure ensured that all data collected from the participants were validated and confirmed for accuracy.

The data collection procedure involves seeking consent of the potential participants to participate in the study. A letter of invitation was electronically mailed to the identified potential participants. As soon as potential participants responded to the invitation, a letter of informed consent was emailed back to the participants. The letter contained the procedures for the face-to-face interview and a written approval of their availability to be interviewed.

Using semi-structured interview questions, the face-to face interview lasted approximately one hour. The questionnaire contained five main questions with the exclusion of the participants' socio-demographic profiles. The socio-demographic profiles included the person's ethnicity, educational attainment, economic status, and age. The semi-structured interview questions contained follow-up questions when clarifications to the responses of the participants were needed. These five main interview questions followed an order aligned to the research questions:

a. Tell me something about your childhood experiences.
b. What is your perception of social morality and religion before and after being affiliated with a gang?
c. What are your childhood, adolescent, and adulthood experiences that shape or facilitate your views about social morality and religion?
d. Please describe your life transformation experiences.
e. What do you think are the most influencing factors that drive this sustained transformation?

Data Analysis

As this grounded theory utilized the Glaserian school of thought, the data analysis utilized the selective coding process of Glaser (1992). Selective coding is a process that is utilized to understand the inductive arguments concerning the phenomenon examined in this present study. In contrast to Strauss' open and axial coding process that viewed the practicality of considering all general variables that can be used to understand a phenomenon, selective coding only selects one core category that relates all other categories emerging from the responses of the participants (Glaser, 1978). Selective coding is a process that focuses on developing a single story from the sub-stories identified by the participants (Glaser, 1978). Glaser believed that concepts of all phenomenon start at a single concept, which become the basis for all other concepts (1992).

While there are differences of views concerning the two schools of grounded method, the coding processes postulated by Glaser and Strauss (1967) possess similar techniques. The Open and Axial coding of Straus and Corbin (1990) has also been described by Glaser as theoretical coding and is considered a valid coding process. Open coding and axial coding are analytical techniques in grounded theory designs. Open coding is the observation and recording process of general themes or categories that emerge from each participant interview or survey document. Strauss and Corbin recommended that researchers start the open coding process by "breaking down, examining, comparing, conceptualizing, and categorizing data" (1990, p. 61), which often occurs in terms of materials and measurements. Researchers sift through gathered data to produce line-by-line codes. Cumbersome but productive, open coding often is advocated in the beginning stages of inquiry as a thorough and systematic analysis of the communication process. The examination of data gathered starts at the word level, and then sequentially examined by phrase, by sentence, and by the entire paragraph. In this process, the examination allows the researcher to uncover any functional relationship between the parts and the whole of entire communicative documents, including surveys and interviews conducted.

Strauss and Corbin (1990) explained that axial coding is the act of relating concepts and categories to each other. Axial coding is an intricate sequence of both inductive and deductive thinking to connect a certain concept to its attributes. For instance, the concept "product need" attributes "user-friendly." Axial coding involves making connections between or "linking" a category and its subcategories (Strauss & Corbin, 1998), which is a combination of inductive and deductive thinking (Glaser & Strauss, 1999). The purpose of axial coding is to reassemble fractured data during open coding (Strauss & Corbin, 1998). Connections between categories include: a) understanding the context in which the phenomenon occurred, b) interactions related to the phenomenon, and c) consequences related to interactions. Axial coding is the beginning step to describe the complex relations between properties as well as, for example, the various ways teachers' reflections informed their practice in context. For data submitted to axial coding, identified categories based on developed codes and the connected code notes from the data refer as most germane to the formulation of research questions.

Although axial and open coding processes were also consistent with the Glaserian grounded theory, this present study utilized the selective coding process developed solely by Glaser (1992). This selective coding process was explored using qualitative analysis software program, such as NVivo by QSR International. The data analysis procedure for the present study was appropriate to analyze the transcribed responses. The NVivo software, however, only facilitated coding of various responses.

Research Methodology

In the application of the basic concept of grounded theory, the researcher employed a thematic analysis on the 14 interviews with the participants. To ensure the validity and reliability of the study, the researcher then made use of a computer software program, NVivo 9 by QSR. The software permitted the researcher to rightly secure the interview transcripts and more significantly ensure the coding process of the gathered data. The researcher then performed the data analysis portion or the thematic analysis of the interviews. Van Manen explained that the goal of thematic analysis is to "uncover themes that are alive in the data" (as cited in Ford, 2007, p. 77). Willig (2013) then added that thematic analysis is a process that "produces knowledge that takes the form of themes, built up from descriptive codes, which capture and make sense of the meanings which characterize the phenomenon under investigation" (p. 65). With these definitions and characteristics, the researcher decided to use the particular method as it was deemed to match the needs of the study. It must be noted that the researcher modified the three basic stages of Attride-Stirling's (2001) to appropriately match this specific research study's method and how the researcher conducted the study. The steps were:

Analysis Stage A: The Reduction or Breakdown of Text

    Step 1. Coding of Material
        (a) Devised a coding framework
        (b) Dissected or divided text into text segments using the coding framework in Step 1a.

    Step 2. Identifying of Themes
        (a) (a) Abstracted themes from coded text segments
        (b) (b) Refined and edited themes

    Step 3. Constructing of Thematic Networks
        (a) Arranged themes
        (b) Selected invariant constituents or the other essential perceptions of the participants
        (c) Rearranged into themes and invariant constituents (with the themes as the ones with the highest responses and the invariant constituents as the ones that followed)
        (d) Illustrated as thematic network (s) or group (s)
        (e) Verified and refined the network (s)

Analysis Stage B: Exploration of Text

    Step 4. Described and explored Thematic Networks or Groups
       (a) Described the network or group
       (b) Explored the network or group

    Step 5. Summarized Thematic Networks or Groups

Analysis Stage C: Integration of Exploration

    Step 6. Interpreted the Patterns (p. 392)

It must be noted that the modification of Attride-Stirling's (2001) steps in data analysis supports the general procedures postulated both by Straus and Corbin (1990) and Glaser in the use of open, axial, and selective coding process. The three-step procedure of Attride-Stirling (2001) may be a recently published procedure, but the concept of identifying codes, establishing thematic networks, and linking the codes to these networks to form a theory were consistent with the established Glaserian method of analysis.

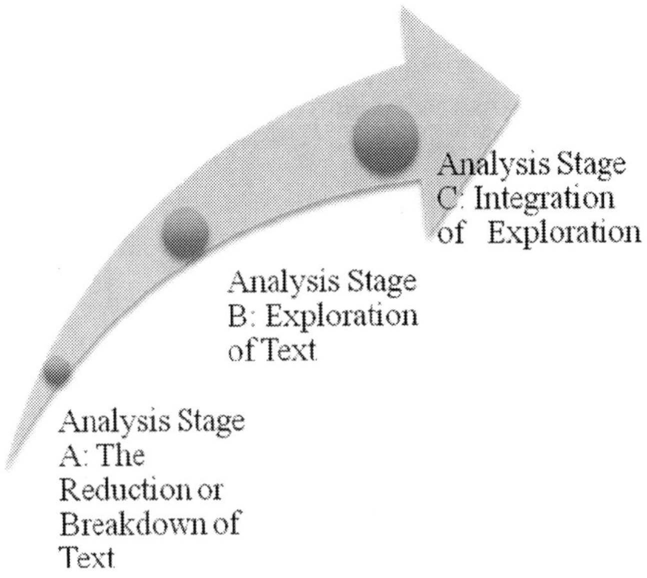

Analysis Stage C: Integration of Exploration

Analysis Stage B: Exploration of Text

Analysis Stage A: The Reduction or Breakdown of Text

Figure 1. Thematic analysis – three basic stages (Attride-Stirling, 2001).

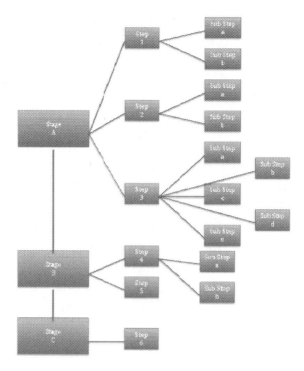

Figure 2. Thematic Networks (Attride-Stirling, 2001).

Reliability

Yin (2009) explains how qualitative data may be considered "non-numerical data – categorical information that can be systematically presented in narrative form (p.11). According to Glaser (1965), a greater concern of open-ended interviews is credibility. Credibility in this study was met through validation of the transcribed interviews. This was done by careful transcription of the recorded interviews which were subsequently sent to the respective participants for peer-checking and validation. This act also addressed confirmability as each participant could confirm the transcription sent to them accurately represented the interview. Erlandson, Harris, Skipper, & Allen (1993) explained how qualitative research must also satisfy dependability. Dependability was met through establishing clear links between research objectives and summary findings (Thomas, 2003).

Validity

In the qualitative paradigm, the idea of trustworthiness indicates a theoretical dependability from which the merit of the research can be assessed (Marshall & Rossman, 1995). This dependability is compared to a qualitative form of reliability and validity used in quantitative research (Brown,

Stevens, Troiano, & Schneider, 2002). Nevertheless, the guiding principles of reliability and validity are unsuitable for grounded theory (Brown et al., 2002). The following general conceptual questions suggested by Strauss and Corbin (1998) were used to evaluate the trustworthiness of the study:

1. Are concepts generated?
2. Are the concepts systematically related?
3. Are there many conceptual linkages, and are the categories well developed? Do categories have conceptual density (richness of the description of a concept)?
4. Is variation within the phenomena built into the theory (how differences are explored, described, and incorporated into the theory)?
5. Are the conditions under which variation can be found built into the study and explained?
6. Has process been taken into account?
7. Do the theoretical findings seem significant, and to what extent?
8. Does the theory stand the test of time and become part of the discussions and ideas exchanged among relevant social and professional groups? (pp. 270-272)

Peer debriefing also supports the credibility of the data in the grounded theory methodology and provides the means for the establishment of the overall trustworthiness of the research findings (Lincoln & Guba, 1985). The strategy known as member checks was conducted for participants to validate the accuracy of the findings and to determine and account for misrepresentation present in the data (Merriam, 2009).

Researcher Biases

One of the initial actions by the researcher in qualitative research and specifically grounded theory is to acknowledge influences that may bias the study (Jones & Alnoy, 2011). By acknowledging researcher bias, the study gains a degree of scientific hardiness (Jones & Alnoy, 2011).

Researcher bias is a pervasive issue (Onwuegbuzie & Leech, 2007). However, even while recognizing that unintended errors still occur in studies despite thorough preventive measures (Mehra, 2002), for the current study caution was used to avoid one of the most pervasive biases, the Hawthorne effect. Landsberger (1958) studied the Hawthorne experiments to try to ascertain the reasoning for the astonishing research outcomes. His work suggested that participants have a tendency to do things to please the researcher and as a result, the research outcomes can be negatively skewed. In an effort to prevent this type of researcher bias, the following were employed.

1. Document all personal biases in a research journal;
2. Determine the source of the personal biases; and

3. Eliminate the interview questions that motivate the participants to agree with the researcher's biases.

Ethical Considerations

The unit of analysis in the study was former gang members who have successfully transformed their lives from gang affiliation to becoming Christians. As such, permission was requested from the participants identified to participate in the study.

The researcher assured the participants that their confidentiality would be maintained until the completion of the study. The researcher also obtained the permission of the participants and ensured that each participant gave consent for the disclosure of the information once the researcher decided to disclose the background information of participants.

A fictitious name system was used to maintain the anonymity of the participants. The researcher assigned each participant a unique identifying name. Fictitious names were assigned in sequential order of interviews to identify the participants prior to each scheduled interview. The information was secured in a password-protected computer file for the duration of the study. All hard copy data were physically secured in a locked file cabinet at the researcher's workstation. All electronic data were stored on a password-protected computer. File cabinets and computer were located in a study room with limited access by individuals other than the researcher. At the conclusion of the three-year data retention stage, all forms and questionnaire data will be shredded and disposed of, including all electronic information being retained on portable media storage devices.

Summary

The purpose of this qualitative grounded theory study was to develop a theory that supports faith-based rehabilitation programs for male adult gang affiliated members. The purposive sample of 14 participants who were: a) male adults between the ages of 21 and 60 years, b) former gang members who attended faith-based programs within churches, and c) able to sustain the life transformation as a result of attending faith-based rehabilitation programs constituted the participants of the study. Themes were identified according to how the interviews raised certain topics related to the phenomenon under study. These themes were identified through the process of open and axial coding (Strauss & Corbin, 1990). The subsequent chapter describes the findings of the study and discusses the implications for social change.

The purpose of this qualitative grounded theory research through a thematic analysis was to explore the application of a faith-based approach to rehabilitation programs based on the experiences and perceptions of males who were former members of community gangs from Latin America, Central America, and the United States living in the United States. The study aimed to produce meaningful perceptions and knowledge from the interview responses and thus, provide an understanding of the role that religion plays in the transformational changes of an individual involved in gang membership. This was also performed to determine the contribution of faith-based rehabilitation programs to the lives of former male gang members from families in Florida, United States. A total of 14 face-to-face and semi-structured interviews, all audio-recorded by the researcher, were conducted with former gang members who were: 1) male adults between the ages of 21 and 60 years, 2) former gang members who attended faith-based programs within churches, and 3) able to sustain the life transformation as a result of attending faith-based rehabilitation programs. The interviews were performed in order to gather information and data straight from those who have directly experienced the life of former gang members.

This chapter also presents the description of the sample population, a brief explanation of the methodology used, and the presentation of findings with the tables and verbatim texts to support the established themes of the study.

— CHAPTER 3 —
Data Analysis and Results

The main sources of the study were the 14 in-depth interviews with the former gang members. The researcher, using the responses of the participants thoroughly analyzed the experiences and perceptions of the former gang members who have transformed their lives and faith through the years.

Research Questions

The data collected by the researcher were all aimed to address the central research question of: What is the role that religion plays in gang membership that results in transformational change of the lives of individuals who were formerly involved in gang criminal behaviors? In addition, the three other research questions have also been fully answered.

> **Research Question 1 (RQ1):** What are the childhood life experiences of the former gang members prior to their involvement with their respective gangs?

> **Research Question 2a (RQ2a):** How do former gang members perceive social morality and the role of religion across different life stages- during their affiliation with a gang?

> **Research Question 2b (RQ2b):** How do former gang members perceive social morality and the role of religion across different life stages- after their affiliation with a gang?

> **Research Question 3 (RQ3):** What are the life-changing events that made former gang members leave their gang affiliations?

Participants of the study were 14 former gang members who were: 1) male adults between the ages of 21 and 60 years, 2) former gang members who attended faith-based programs within churches, and

3) able to sustain the life transformation as a result of attending faith-based rehabilitation programs. The breakdown of the demographics sample can be referred to in Table 1.

Adam was 60 years old during the time of the interview. He is a White/ American who graduated from college. Currently he is a Senior Pastor in Florida.

Albert was 32 years old during the time of the interview. He is also a Hispanic/American who finished the secondary level of education (high school graduate). Currently he is in the warehousing business in California.

Roman was 60 years old during the time of the interview. He is a Latino/Nicaraguan and reached the elementary of education. Currently he is a maintenance building manager in Florida.

Jacob was 40 years old during the time of the interview. He is a Hispanic/American and had a middle school education. Currently he is a minister at a Recovery House in Florida.

Elijah was 45 years old during the time of the interview. He is a Hispanic/ American and finished education at the college level. Currently he is an IT assistant engineer in Florida.

Martin was 40 years old during the time of the interview. He is a White/ American who reached the secondary level of education or the high school level. Currently he is a facilities manager in Tennessee.

Angel was 31 years old during the time of the interview. He is a Black/American who reached the secondary level of education or the high school level as well. Currently he is a landscaper in Florida.

Jeremiah was 36 years old during the time of the interview. He is a White/American who finished the college level and completed his education. Currently he is a missionary pastor in Ecuador for a church in Florida.

Efraim was 30 years old during the time of the interview. He is a Black/American who successfully reached the college level of education. Currently he is an IT programmer in Florida.

Umberto was 39 years old during the time of the interview. He is a Latino/Argentine who reached the college level of education. Currently he is an outreach director in Florida.

Gabriel was 38 years old during the time of the interview. He is a Latino/Ecuadorian who reached the high school level of education. Currently he is the Director of a Peace Youth Foundation in Guatemala for a church in Florida.

Peter was 29 years old during the time of the interview. He is also a Black Latino/Ecuadorian who reached the high school level of education. Currently he is the Sub-Director of a Peace Youth Foundation in Guatemala for a church in Florida.

Manfred was 45 years old during the time of the interview. He is a White/American who reached the high school level of education. Currently he is the assistant resident director for a Bible training center in Florida.

Anibal was 27 years old during the time of the interview. He is a White/American who successfully completed the college level of education. Currently he is an assistant resident staff for a Bible training center in Florida.

Table 1

Participants' Socio-Demographics Profiles

Fictitious Name	Age	Ethnicity	Education Level	Occupation
Adam	60	White	College	Senior Pastor
Albert	32	Hispanic	High School	Warehousing
Roman	60	Latino	Elementary	Maintenance Building Manager
Jacob	40	Hispanic	Middle School	Minister of a Recovery House
Elijah	45	Hispanic	College	IT Assistant Engineer
Martin	40	White	High school	Facilities Manager
Angel	31	Black	High School	Landscaper
Jeremiah	36	White	College	Missionary Pastor in Ecuador
Efraim	30	Black	College	IT Programmer
Umberto	39	Latino	College	Outreach Director
Gabriel	38	Latino	High School	Director of a Peace Youth Foundation in Guatemala
Peter	29	Black/ Latino	High School	Sub-Director of a Peace Youth Foundation in Guatemala
Manfred	45	White	High School	Assistant Resident Director of Bible Training Center
Anibal	27	White	College	Assistant Resident Staff of Bible Training Center

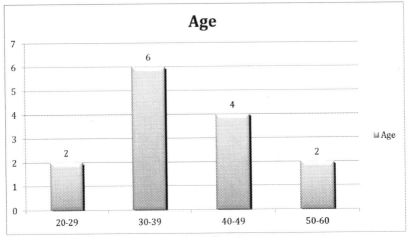

Figure 3. Participants' socio-demographic profiles: Age.

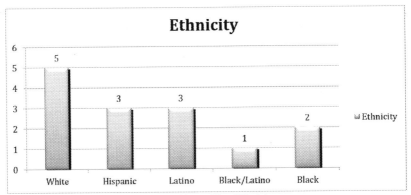

Figure 4. Participants' socio-demographic profiles: Ethnicity.

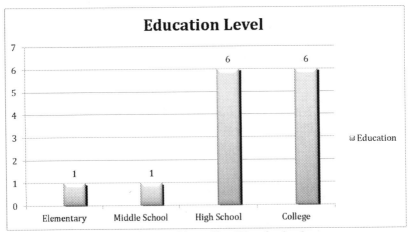

Figure 5. Participants' socio-demographic profiles: Education level.

— CHAPTER 4 —
Thematic Analysis 1

Chapters four through seven, discussed the qualitative thematic analysis of the interviews gathered by the researcher. The researcher found that: the former gang members had a 1) Normal childhood until growing up, some issues and problems emerged. These participants also had 2) No morality and religion, out of control and negative behavior towards other individuals before and during their gang affiliations. Meanwhile, they shared that after, their 3) Religion or faith produced good results overall as an individual and for the other people around them. Lastly, the former gang members decided to transform as they realized that they 4) had to change for their whole family and children to have the image and presence of a father.

Theme 1. Normal childhood until growing up, some issues and problems emerged.

For the first theme that emerged from the first research question which explored the childhood life experiences of the former gang members prior to their involvement with their respective gangs, it was known that the participants had: Normal childhood until growing up, some issues and problems emerged. This theme was deduced from six invariant constituents (including the main theme) and is presented in Table 2. The first theme of the former gang members—sharing that they had a normal childhood until they reached a stage where issues and problems emerged and they could not handle such stress and problems anymore—received the highest number of responses of seven out of the 14 participants or 50% of the total sample population.

Table 2

The Childhood Life Experiences of the Former Gang Members Prior to Their Involvement with Their Respective Gangs

Invariant Constituents	# of occurrences	% of occurrences
Normal childhood until growing up, some issues and problems emerged	7	50%
Experienced violence, trauma/ abuse, and disdain inside their own homes	3	21%
Experienced unconditional love from their mother	2	14%
Raised by a strict father wherein work was their number one priority and nothing else	1	7%
Various background experiences with constant transfers in different neighborhoods	1	7%
Child soldier therefore was exposed early to actions that were not meant for his age	1	7%

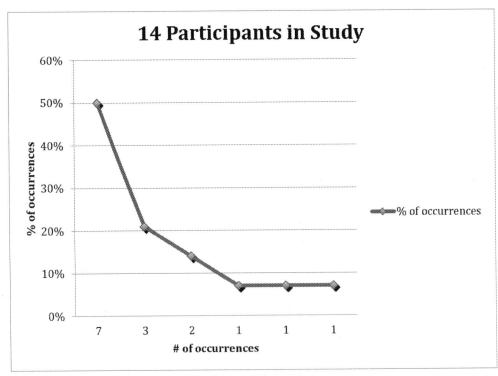

Figure 6. Graph representation of Table 2 – Theme 1.

Overall, the theme that received the most responses from the participants was that they experienced: Normal childhood until growing up, some issues and problems emerged. The participants shared the following.

Martin stated that his childhood was happy until the time came that he had his own opinions and disagreements with his father emerged:

> Martin: When I was little, I was a happy little kid. As I got a little older, I began to have my own opinion. My father and I didn't see eye to eye, so that's kind of when it went downhill at home.

Jeremiah also shared that his childhood was fairly normal; however, he had an alcoholic father. He added that his childhood was mainly composed of playing baseball and truly excelled in the field:

> Jeremiah: I grew up in the suburbs and growing up in a home where my father is an alcoholic. I grew up on the softball field with a bunch of drunks and a hardworking mom that tried to hold the family together and deal with the alcoholic dad and worked like a dog and brought me and my family as much as she could to church every Sunday. I was thinking of following the whole baseball career and that became who I was and what I was defined as was a baseball player. My father ended up at some point becoming sober when I was at the age of 13 and my game that was pretty much it, baseball and I became a baseball star. In many cases for my family and ended up growing up in a decent home, I wasn't abused. I've never lived, we didn't live below poverty, just a suburb type living.
>
> I lived in the same city for my whole entire life, I would say, probably within a five-mile radius, all of my elementary, junior high school and high school years and I would say that was my upbringing. I was very popular in school because of the sports and was able to make friends and you know, I knew many people growing up and I was pretty much a hothead, you know, sports guy.

Umberto stated that he had a normal childhood growing up wherein both his parents were very loving. However, given the nature of his father's occupation he was away most of the time from their family:

> Umberto: I have a very loving father, very loving mother. They are strict. We moved here, we came here from Argentina when I was very small. I could say that my childhood experiences were great. I had some really awesome experiences. My father being very ... He's in the aviation business. He was away a lot. I kind of didn't have a lot of that father figure in my house.

Gabriel shared that he had a normal childhood wherein he had a mother and a stepfather, and everything developed in a normal way:

> Gabriel: Well, my experiences have been like any other kid. There was nothing out of the extraordinary. I studied. My mother, my father was my stepfather, not my biological father. Nothing happened. Everything was ok. Everything developed in a normal way.

Peter added that his experiences were normal as a child; however, the time came when he wanted attention and felt that his family was not there for him:

> Peter: Well, basically the experiences I have of my childhood they are good, a little before my adolescence, because my parents will take care of giving us everything to me and my brothers. But, suddenly I felt like a lack of love, of caring, my father was working, my mom busy, and therefore, I found myself in the adolescence, nobody to share my things with, so I felt like a stranger with my family.

Manfred stated that he was raised normally as a child and even had a Catholic background but then encountered issues and troubles growing up:

> Manfred: I was raised Catholic. I went to a private Catholic school through 8th grade. I didn't get in much trouble then. It was just through high school years that I started getting in trouble. I was an altar boy in Catholic Church. My basic foundation of God was formed back then, before I really even knew Him.

Anibal added that his childhood was normal and good wherein he was able to receive what he needed:

> Anibal: I grew up with a great childhood, a pretty well to do family. My mother was a fashion designer for dance wears; so you grow up at the ice rink ... she made figure skating outfits. My father was a dockworker. My mother was the moneymaker; my father was just a hard worker. I have an older brother, older sister ... both doing really well right now.
> Childhood was great. I had no wants; everything I needed I had. Looked up to my brother a lot. He was kind of the guy I would go to. We were close; we weren't real close. He was kind of like my idol, I would say. He played hockey, I wanted to play hockey. He went out and partied, I wanted to party. I kind of grew up in that kind of ... It was a good childhood though.

The second invariant constituent or essential experience that followed the first theme was that three out of the 14 participants or 21% of the total sample population: Experienced violence, trauma/abuse, and disdain inside their own homes. The participants shared the following.

Albert stated that he experienced violence inside his own home and abandonment from his father as well. Another experience was the trauma and negative influences within the community, which had a great effect in his behavior:

> Albert: As a child, I've experienced violence in my home. I experienced being neglected at home. I experienced, also, drug abuse, alcohol abuse. I experienced abandonment by my father. Not just to name the bad things… I experienced traumas. I lived in an area that was very crucial. At the age of five, I lived in the downtown Los Angeles area. I witnessed murder scenes. I witnessed the environment that was heavily influenced by drugs and drug dealings, and gangs. Based on that influence, it took part in my behavior.
>
> I would say, first of all, my eyes, my mind, my life was exposed to such things, and to such violence, and those lessons really just influenced me in a negative way where I was attracted to those things. For example, I would say, I seen my father hitting my mother. Growing up, I did the same thing. I saw my father coming home intoxicated with alcohol. Therefore, I did the same thing.

Jacob stated that he experienced abuse as a child:

> Jacob: I'm from a large family. Extended family is large. Lots of cousins. Was abused as a child from the ages of, as far as I can remember, 4 to 8. Grew up down here in Pompano Beach, but I was born in the Boston area.
>
> As I mentioned in the first question, the abuse. Seeing abuse in my family as well, my other siblings. Seeing a lot of violence growing up. That tremendously shaped my perspective.

Angel shared his story of how his parents' problems and fighting affected him as a kid and because of their aggression he would get physically hurt from their fights:

> Angel: Yes, my childhood, growing up it was very hard and difficult because both of my parents, they were alcoholic and most of the time I would find myself, when they fight, when my parents start fighting, I would find myself, maybe I would run, go to the beach with my friends and stay there until midnight and come home when everything was over but when I came home I would get in trouble and get beat.

Severely with my mom and my dad and then the same thing was happen again and I would run, go hang out with my friend whole day, you know, and then come back home but it was because I was really did not want to be like involved in it. You know, because when they got drunk, we get hurt from that. So, and it was very difficult.

The third invariant constituent or essential experience that followed the first theme was that two out of the 14 participants or 14% of the total sample population: Experienced unconditional love from their mother. The participants shared the following.

Albert shared that despite the negative experiences, he also had great memories from the love that his mother gave and showed him:

Albert: But I've also experienced the love from my mother, the encouragement of my mother, the courage of my mother, the braveness of my mother, the boldness of my mother.

Roman stated that his childhood was normal until his parents separated. This event made him closer to his mother and when his mother transferred to another place, this affected him negatively:

Roman: Well, my childhood was very normal, until my parents got separated. My father gave my mother a very tough life, so she had to get divorced. I was looking at that but at the same time, not that it hurt me, but it made me be closer to my mother. So, when she found herself without her husband and my father, my mother told us that because she didn't have any wealth to provide us with, I have to give you an education. I want you to study, be prepared, and it doesn't matter how much it will cost me. You will have to help yourself that this happens. And that's why each of us picked up their careers and I studied, but as I told you before, I was the lazy one, the black sheep of the family.

And then I started my childhood when my mom moved from Legon to the capital, and I stayed with my grandma, in Nicaragua. I then started to see life in such a sad way, being far from my mom due to circumstances out of her control, living with my great grandmother, and sometimes we didn't have anything to eat. And that's how I went on growing, she died, I studied like I told you very little, but the classes were strong ones, the mind opened on anyone, teachers were really good. And then I started to live my life working at that tiny age.

The fourth invariant constituent or essential experience that followed the first theme was that one out of the 14 participants or 7% of the total sample population was: Raised by a strict father wherein work was his number one priority and nothing else. The participant shared the following.

Adam stated that his childhood mainly consisted of having to work for his father all the time and being with other children and other normal activities were somehow overlooked by the need to follow the demands of his father:

> Adam: Unlike most kids, I didn't have summer vacations I worked every day, Saturdays, during school year, Christmas vacation, Easter vacation, and then until... not so much after school but when I turned 14 then it was after school every day also because we moved our store close to our house. Right in front of us a matter of fact. From that time on... Then at 16 my dad coerced me rightfully so, to drop out of high school. I only completed the tenth grade and for legitimate reason, he had to have surgery and I was the only one who could run the business and he be out of commission a while so I dropped out at that point.
>
> Family. Father dominated, 100%. Good man. Hardworking man. He ruled. That was it. For instance, working, it was not knowing never a choice, it was never brought up that I had a choice. That was it. It was just, "For now you're working. That's it."
>
> Every day the thing that I miss the most... all my buddies will be out playing as a little kid, they have summers, they can stay home watch TV, I never had that. I had my mother and two younger sisters they took care of the household. Me and my dad took care of the work part. Lots of times I wouldn't see my mother all day long because we go to work fairly early, at eight o'clock, and lots of times we wouldn't get home until eight o'clock, six days a week.
>
> Christmas time, you could forget it. From the day I was one guy ... I love Christmas but I hated the Christmas season because in the business we were in from the day after Thanksgiving until even Christmas Eve ... lot of nights would ... twelve o'clock at night we're still working because it's so busy selling bicycles.

The fifth invariant constituent or essential experience that followed the first theme was that one out of the 14 participants or 7% of the total sample population had: Various background experiences with constant transfers in different neighborhoods. The participant shared the following.

Elijah stated that as a child he had various experiences from good to bad neighborhoods but remembered that he would always be afraid at night for his safety and security:

> Elijah: My childhood experiences varied because we moved a lot as a child. We moved from bad neighborhoods to better neighborhoods as my father's and mother's occupation stabilized, but I remember at very young living in the harshest part of Chicago area where it was very common to live without utilities sometimes or the luxuries of life. As in luxuries I would mean three square meals a day, TV and toys. I remember things like that, and really the security. I remember at night being afraid a lot.

The sixth invariant constituent or essential experience that followed the first theme was that one out of the 14 participants or 7% of the total sample population was a: child soldier therefore was exposed early to actions that were not meant for his age. The participant shared the following.

Efraim stated that he grew up as a child soldier wherein by the age of eight, he was already seeing things that he was not supposed to witness as a very young kid:

> Efraim: It was interesting… interesting. Grew up as a child soldier by the age of 8, very interesting. I don't know how specific it would be but I thought it was interesting as a child soldier. I experienced a lot of things that I didn't think was meant for an 8-year-old kid to experience at the time so very interesting.

— CHAPTER 5 —
Thematic Analysis 2

Theme 2. No morality and religion, out of control and negative behavior towards other individuals.

The second theme that emerged from the second research question (a) which was how former gang members perceive social morality and the role of religion across different life stages-during their affiliations with the gang, it was known that they believed that there was: No morality and religion, out of control and negative behavior towards other individuals. This was deduced from five invariant constituents (including the main theme) which can be seen in Table 3. The second theme of the former gang members sharing that before and during their gang affiliations they believed that morality and religion did not exist and had out of control behaviors; this received the highest number of responses with four responses out of the 14 participants or 29% of the total sample population.

Table 3
How Former Gang Members Perceive Social Morality and the Role of Religion across Different Life Stages- During Their Affiliation with the Gang

Invariant Constituents	# of occurrences	% of occurrences
No morality and religion, out of control and negative behavior towards other individuals	4	29%
No morality and religion, feeling that they could justify anything and everything- good or bad actions	3	21%
No morality, only fear and religion was not real	3	21%
Belief that God is always there even in the negative actions and mistakes they were making	3	21%
No morality and religion as a drug addict and there was emptiness within the individual	1	7%

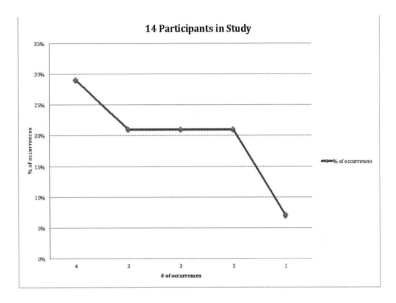

Figure 7. Graph representation of Table 3 – Theme 2.

Overall, the second theme that received the most responses from the participants was that they perceived: No morality and religion because of their out of control and negative behavior towards other individuals. The participants shared the following.

Albert stated that his behavior was not good at all especially when it came to social morality and religion:

> Albert: The social morality, the behavior that I had was somewhat out of control. It was a very negative behavior. Rebellion, aggressive and violent. It's due to the fact of what I was exposed to or what I seen at home, what I seen around in the neighborhood, or what I seen in my own home, in the apartment buildings that I lived. My behavior was a negative one, was one of selfish one. The influence of friends that I also socialized with had the same type of backgrounds with their parents in their own homes.
>
> Therefore, my behavior was not good at all. I was just truly a child with problems. That was before the faith.

Jacob also added the same experience wherein as a member of a gang, morality was totally not present for him during that time. He even shared that he was destructive as a person:

Jacob: Well, ironically, as a child during that timeframe which I spoke of in the first question, I had an encounter with God. My family was Christian, and I remember a presence of God in my life even at that age. So morality, I always held a high value on morality, but before or while I was involved in the gang activity, I was not adhering to those, those viewpoints. And because of that I did always have the sense of guilt because of it, but I didn't adhere to those moralities that were kind of ingrained in me. Afterward, after my gang experience, I got into; deep into drugs so my morality wasn't ... I still didn't adhere to those perspectives, those views on morality.

I was lashing out with anger, outwardly. And it was fixated on other people and there came a point in time when that became something that I didn't really want to do anymore. That just wasn't appealing to me anymore and I was really repulsed by it. But, I became inwardly destructive. And I began to do more drugs and more alcohol and got very depressed at different times or different seasons or times in my life.

Jeremiah stated that morality for him was based on the environment he constantly was in; growing up in Las Vegas somehow made him believe that immoral acts were normal and that religion was just for adults and serious individuals:

Jeremiah: I would say that, you know, your reality determines your perception in the aspect of morality was what I was shown with a fixed point of view and you know, growing up in the environment that I grew up in, you know there's a lot of things that was okay to do, you know, drinking and making money and you know, success was you know, being able to do those things was all a part of my morality if you will. This is what you're supposed to do.

Well before, you know, my world, because I grew up in Las Vegas was, basically there were two worlds. There was the world of, you know, at home and then there was a world outside of home which was a lifestyle of the strip of Las Vegas, casinos and strip clubs, you know, I was a very, very young age so my world was very different. So I looked at religion as being, you know, a different world. The other world that Vegas had was, you know, it was two different worlds. This is what was fun, this is what was exciting and this is what the real people of the world did. The religion was for the boring, for the duds, for the people that wanted to live a safe and strict life.

Manfred stated that there was a point in his life when his behavior towards others was negative and out of control:

Manfred: Okay, let me think. A big changeover in my life happened when I went from the private school to a city school, where I didn't know anybody. I didn't have a lot of friends in high school, so that's where I fell into that group of people at that time. In the '80s where I grew up in Alabama, there was a lot of racism, and we fell into that group. When I was with that group, that's where my lack of morals, I would say, about respecting people, regardless of their background or ethnic background; that's whenever it really started progressing, to be of a hate, violent thing. In that time in the early '80s, it was really bad, where I was from. At the age of 25, I entered the mission, Restoration Ranch in Alabama. That was another of the life changing moments, where I come to understand a relationship with Christ, and he took all that from me.

The second invariant constituent or essential experience that followed the second theme was that three out of the 14 participants or 21% of the total sample population had: No morality and religion, feeling that they could justify anything and everything—good or bad actions. The participants shared the following.

Adam stated that he had the confidence that he could justify any action he did and that he could get away with anything. He even shared that before the transformation he did not have a social security number but owned a business, as an example of getting away with his responsibilities:

Adam: Before there were certain things I would limit myself from but not many things. I consider myself fairly moral but my biggest thing was I could justify anything, and even things I didn't normally do if I found a justification for it in my mind, it would be. Just like that. Sometimes I do things I'd even disappoint myself. I said, "I thought I wouldn't do these kind of things," but I did.

Before that I didn't even take out a social security number and I owned a business, I own a big house and one of my uncles is an accountant, I asked him to do my books he says, "Are you crazy? We'll both go to jail." But he put me with another guy and I was about 26 years old and the man sits down and he says, "Okay, let's get started."

Efraim stated that during the time that he was part of an affiliation, he felt and believed that he had the power to do anything he wanted to:

Efraim: It changes because at the time it felt like I had the power to do whatever I wanted to because I had a gun, so my perception was, "Hey I have a gun, so I could do whatever I wanted to." No one had power to tell me what to do or what not to do so I did what I wanted to and so morality, it wasn't given. It was mine whatever I wanted to do at the time.

Umberto added that both morality and religion were non-existent for him, being a rebel at a very young age, he thought that everything was okay and that doing immoral acts were normal:

> Umberto: I would say before religion wasn't really real to me. I mean, it was kind of a myth, kind of like put in, kind of like Disney World kind of deal. Just a bunch of fairy tales and it was just a place that we went to once a year.
>
> I don't really ... To be perfectly honest with you, I didn't know any different from a religion perspective and a secular perspective, any morality. It was no difference to me.
>
> Well, I would say I come from that skater background, so we were skaters. That's one thing I left out. You could call that a gang. We were just all about rebelling, sex, drugs and rock and roll, and we don't give a rip who sees it. We just didn't care.

The third invariant constituent or essential experience that followed the second theme was that another three out of the 14 participants or 21% of the total sample population had: No morality and believed that only fear and religion was not real. The participants shared the following.

Elijah stated that before leaving the gang there was no morality only for other people, yet at the same time he perceived that religion was for punishment:

> Elijah: My presumptions of morality was that there was no morality there was only fear because people respected the fact that you were affiliated with a membership of an organization or a club or a team of people that had no morality. It means they had no rules and when there's no rules that means that the retaliation is limitless. I learned early on that, to help my family to sleep better, it help that we were affiliated or that I was affiliated with the neighborhood and community, which was predominantly gang-based according to your ethnicity. It depended on where or also dependent on what part geographically the neighborhood you lived on.
>
> The role of religion was, at first, pretty much only for the adults and there was a punishment. I remember religion was looked at upon as the do not's. Do not do this or do not do that because if you do, you do one of the do not's, then you're not going to like what you get. Religion was always accompanying with punishment. I learn that the lack of morality didn't come with punishment all the time. It came with freedom, temporary freedom as long as you didn't get caught.

Martin shared that morality is an emotional topic for him as well as religion as it involves the memories of his father:

Martin: Before, I didn't pay much attention to religion. Morality... to me this was an emotional one. When I showed my emotions from a religion standpoint, from what I saw from my father at home, was exactly opposite from what I'd ever heard. It made me not want anything to do with religion because what I saw in him I thought, "Why in the world would I want to be part of that if that's what you become?"

Like I said, my father was big in church, and at times he was even a pastor at a church, but yet ... And of course I would be dragged, not physically dragged, dragged to church. I would listen to what he said, and I would see what he would do, and I thought to myself, "If this is what religion looks like, I want no part of it."

Peter stated that morality was not present for him and that religion was not real as it was mostly for the priests who wanted financial resources:

Peter: Before I saw religion like something where people would go to with the Catholic theme to confess their sins, and ...I don't know... the priests would take advantage monetarily, I saw it right? And later, when I was in the group, problems started to arise and I said to myself: "well if I look for something from this earth, someone whom to confess with, whom to tell my problems to, then one suddenly starts thinking about God, and one reflects: "why? Why to me? God help me." Then one realizes that there is something more, right? That there is a celestial being to whom we owe Him life and many more things, more so, all the creation.

Well...what I can see is that I put myself always in the day-to-day. There are a lot of people that are within, let's say, the politics. Those are people that steal all they want but however, here comes the dedicated parent, who steals a chicken and they are the first ones who are condemned for being thieves. But things are not always like that, "it's said that the rope doesn't break from the thinnest end."

The fourth invariant constituent or essential experience that followed the second theme was that another three out of the 14 participants or 21% of the total sample population had a: Belief that God is always there even in the negative actions and mistakes they were making. The participants shared the following.

Angel stated that although he was making mistakes and actions against God's will he has always been exposed to God and His vitality in peoples' lives:

Angel: For me, I think religion played a very significant role in my life. At the age of, I was five years old and I got baptized in a Methodist church and my parents used to go to that church but I never went often but when I went, things that I learned from there, I think they make me to be, you know, it gave me a mind of, you know, God is always there, that God is always protecting, that God is always want my best. So all those things got stuck in my mind and even though it was hard, even though I was doing things that I wasn't supposed to do but those things brought me back to the straight and narrow, just to be... So, you know, I think religion played a significant role in my life in that, yes, part of it.

Gabriel shared that even if he had actions that were not proper, he has always believed that God was present and that religion was there:

Gabriel: Well, we always had religion, and the first most important thing was God. We always placed God as a supreme being to protect us who will help us with any difficulty or problem. So, before and after...it is having to answer to God, though some actions we have, we don't act the right way, you understand? I had actions or did not act the right way in the past.

Anibal stated that he always feared God and believed that he was present despite the negative acts he was doing:

Anibal: My sense of morality before is you can be a good person as long as you don't hurt somebody. You should always respect your parents, don't steal ... basically the Ten Commandments, even though I didn't live up to the Ten Commandments ... but that was my ideal. You can do that and you'll live a good life.

Afterwards it changed a little bit, but I still always thought I was a good person. I didn't hurt anybody, physically. I stole from a bunch of people, I robbed people, and I did everything to please myself. Social morality ... I kind of had a view of, a Friedrich Nietzsche kind of view, almost "Will to Power," or Karl Marx religion is "the opiate of the masses." It holds people down rather than freeing people. If you believe in something blindly, how are you going to strive for something that you don't understand if you just accept something blindly?

I always felt that religion is holding people back from what they truly can become. That was my view all throughout college until basically I got to where I am here.

The fifth invariant constituent or essential experience that followed the second theme was that another one out of the 14 participants or 7% of the total sample population had: No morality and religion as a drug addict and there was emptiness within the individual. The participant shared the following.

Roman shared that he was a drug addict for 30 years and was a leader and a politician of a large party; however, there was always emptiness within him:

Roman: Well, in my case, I could understand this until 1974, moment where the only spirit, Christ spirit, reached me and took me to a church. Do you understand? Do you understand what I mean? Because, in 1974, I had to travel to Managua to the North side of Nicaragua where I lived with a family of mine after the big earthquake. Then, and…

Then I was 17 years old-20 years old and started to work on the same thing, in mechanic. But someone saw me…the ones that belonged to the movement, and they recruited me. And, I became a politic leader to the masses, without studying anything. I had such a persuasion that engaged many and then to recruit them to the movement. But in all that time, so you have an idea, I was a drug addict for 30 years, even being in the military, even being a diplomat, because I was a diplomat. I went to Madrid, Mexico, Venezuela, Panama, you understand? But there was emptiness, emptiness, and I was trying to fill that emptiness… and I couldn't. There is always emptiness, in society as well as in the human being, and no matter how many solutions we look for to fill that emptiness, there is none, but only through religion, and to me, through Christ.

— CHAPTER 6 —
Thematic Analysis 3

Theme 3. Religion or faith produced good results overall as an individual and for the other people around them.

The third theme that emerged from the second research question (b) which was how former gang members perceive social morality and the role of religion across different life stages-after their affiliations with the gang, it was known that: Religion or faith produced good results overall as an individual and for the other people around them. It was deduced from three invariant constituents (including the main theme) and can be seen in Table 4. The third theme of the former gang members sharing that after leaving their gangs, their religion and faith increased and even produced good effects in their lives received the highest number of responses with seven out of the 14 total sample population or 50%.

Table 4
How Former Gang Members Perceive Social Morality and the Role of Religion across Different Life Stages – After Their Affiliation with the Gang

Invariant Constituents	# of occurrences	% of occurrences
Religion or faith produced good results overall as an individual and for the other people around them	7	50%
Growing closer to God stopped the immoral acts and changed their behaviors completely	6	43%
Belief that being part of a gang was not moral thus allowed God to change him	1	7%

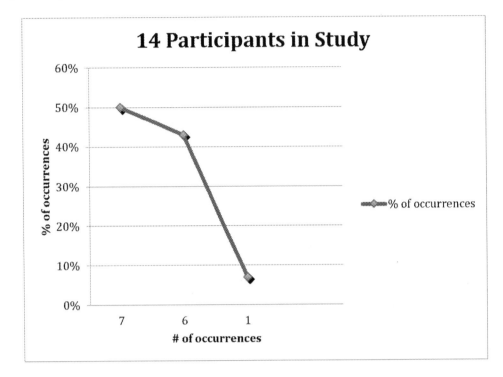

Figure 8. Graph representation of Table 4 – Theme 3.

Overall, the third theme that received the most responses from the participants was that they believe that: Religion or faith produced good results overall as an individual and for the other people around them. The participants shared the following.

Elijah stated that he believes that after his gang affiliations, morality and religion had good meaning and effect not only for him but his family members as well:

> Elijah: That would be about 15 years and I still considered myself in a faith-based program so I don't believe that I'll ever leave as a faith-based program because the things I learned about as a child show themselves to be faithful and the principles have produced good results not only in my life in the life of my children and it kept my children out of gangs and my friends that are in gangs, the reason they write me is because they write me to celebrate me that they admired the fact that someone they know actually really did it and they want to know the secret and I'm more than happy to share with them.

Martin stated that after leaving the gang he did not think even once of going back as religion played a big role and that having morals and God in his life were greater than anything:

Martin: Because what better life to live than one for Christ? It sounds, I guess, stupid. Some people find their quote, unquote "idols" in making a lot of money, or having nice clothes, shoes, and cars, whatever. I think for people like myself, the idol is the adrenaline rush or the destruction of something ... someone, whatever the case may be. Those things are what my heart longed for ... to just cause hell everywhere that I had went.

> When I had gotten saved and went through the ministry ... I want to honor God and to spread His love and His light, and that's where true joy comes from. The other ones ... from the seemingly okay ones to society, to the ones that I lived were all temporary. For a moment, I was satisfied ... and I had to do it again, and I had to do it again, and I had to do it again, and I had to do it again. I have a God that loves me just as I am, and why would I not want to share that with someone else?

Angel added that after leaving the gang, he went back to the church and from then on only had good and positive thoughts and paths as an individual:

> Angel: I live by church now and I work by church so I'm always around a good environment and my dad's a pastor here at the church so I'm always around something. So it's got my mind going to a place for good path and I'm not perfect but I'm positive. I like not to really think about those bad things anymore.

Umberto shared that after his transformation and affiliation with the gang, he started to believe that he owed the people accountability and transparency. That being honest with others as the Bible taught is much needed:

> Umberto: I would say my love life with my wife is amazing, and that supports me so much. Like everything. My wife supports me. Like she works with me. This is her office here. She's part of the Outreach with me. I have accountability partners in case something or I become an idiot. I got people I can go and talk to. I got friends that pray for me. I've got this family, man. It's very similar to what I had because I still skate. I am still involved in skateboarding. You can go and checkout the skate park. I'm still involved. I'm loving on the culture that I used to be, but I'm not the same person. That's another thing that's very important for me to get the support and to sustain myself in a spiritual...
>
> The Bible says to be above reproach. I think that's what really gets me to... drives me to really be accountable, to really be transparent with people, and to make sure I'm doing what I need to be doing. Every Tuesday I'm doing Bible studies.

You know what I used to hate the most? I used to hate the most in the past, and the best, when you know you have teachers and they tell you, be good, don't do drugs, whatever, whatever. Then you'd run into them at the bar Shooters and they were just hammered. We got one guy that, he used to drill us and then he got DUI. You know what I mean? Like stuff like that.

Gabriel stated that after leaving the gang, he realized that helping and being a good individual overall with God as the center was more fulfilling than his old lifestyle:

Gabriel: That I am at ease, I live a quiet life, I don't have problems with anybody, I have a job, I can earn the bread of each day for me and my family. I can help other boys that work with me, we have created other sources of work, and it is like a type of change. And we are working in what we like.

Peter stated that after seeing the changes, he perceived morality and religion to be positive to the whole society:

Peter: Because they brought too many problems to my life! And all the positive I have until today has been possible for the evolution we could do within the gang towards society. As a matter of fact, when you were referred as being in a gang, you thought about being a drug trafficker, a rapist, a killer, and all of that! So with the work we did we could help society to change their minds and say different things about us, correct?

By interviews, through pictures by Internet so nobody can call us delinquents. If you can put all the positive things we did during the world soccer championship in South Africa or go to another country and say I am part of a youth foundation, and the change we've been through in such a way that we can help others so they can also have this perception and change other's perception of us.

Anibal stated that after his gang affiliations he saw the importance of faith and how it can duly change one person or an individual:

Anibal: My desire not to want to go back to where I was. My desire to know God. My entire life I've had an intellectual thing to try to ... I've always been interested in religions. I was always interested in how religion can drive people. And faith ... in blind faith. That always intrigued me, saying, "How can you believe this when you can't see, feel, touch." If you can't test something, if you can't have a hypothesis and prove, "Alright, this is the result. I see this." How can you just believe in something?

The second invariant constituent or essential experience that followed the third theme was that six out of the 14 participants or 43% of the total sample population believed that: Growing closer to God stopped the immoral acts and changed their behaviors completely. The participants shared the following.

Adam stated that with his newfound relationship with God then, he started to realize the mistakes that he committed and one by one began to fix them as well. He shared that he started to pay his taxes and went on straight and honest after the transformation:

> Adam: After I was born again those things ... some of them immediately and obviously in the process of growing closer to God stopped and that's it. Only by the spirit of God because my idea of it was completely different.
>
> For instance, sexual morality, I didn't think much of before that after that that was a no-no. I didn't really pay my taxes, after I got saved, the Bible says, "Render unto Caesar what was due to Caesar," I pay every dime of tax. A matter of fact I've been audited and I come out squeaky clean years ago. A matter of fact they came and apologize to me. They kept my books for a year and it says, "You are way above board." I say, "Yeah," and that's it.
>
> Even at that point I started paying taxes but not everything I'm supposed to. It was until years later when I actually came to God and then I drew the line at that ... saw a whole different perspective.

Albert added that after seeing his faith in Jesus Christ, his behavior started changing for the better and the light guided him into the right path:

> Albert: After a faith, when I received Christ, that behavior started changing. Even though before I knew it was wrong, just the influence, based on what I'd seen, and what I'd seen in my home. To me it was normal. I mean; I understood it was bad, but I stood behind to do the things that it was not that bad.
>
> But after the faith and after receiving Christ, all those behaviors and all those years that I lived, I started to realize, I started to see the total mess that I truly was, the total ... Negative person that I was, and the bad behavior that I conducted myself with, the disrespect to the teachers at schools, to my brothers, to my friends... The crimes that I committed, the deaths that I committed. After the faith, I would say

that God was breaking me out of bondage and placing me into a light, and showing me the lack of light without Christ in my life.

Roman stated that God liberated him from the addiction and negative acts and after he was able to realize which is the true religion from God's words:

Roman: Well, to me probably was a negative thing, what is religion, which is something negative and destructive and we see so many examples, and God liberated me from that, now I know which is the true religion, which is spoken in the Gospel. The peace, love, joy, and most of all that you are secluded to live for God. There is a 180-degree change of who I was, to what I am now.

Jeremiah stated that he always believed that God was with him pushing him to change and be a better person. One day he allowed God in and transformation for the better happened:

Jeremiah: You know, I believe it was just the grace of God and, you know, pursuing Him and continuing with Him and getting to know Him and for Him to, He just filled my life and recognizing that there was no going back and just getting better and that He has just a wonderful plan for me and you know, the big statement I want to say is that, you know, walking by faith with the Lord, today I can say that, you know, eight years ago my wildest dream would never match what I'm doing today and so, I mean, the truth of it is simply that be faithful, you know, be faithful to Him and, you know, He really, when He says He has a plan, it's a journey.

Efraim was unaware at first that religion was working for him; however, he then allowed the relationship with God to form and believed in the changes it may bring to his life:

Efraim: Even though I knew that my adoptive parents were Christian at the time, and my biological parents were Christian, but I really didn't know what it meant to have a relationship with God. So the transformation came when God allowed me to be part of a family that took me in, really took care of me, to say, "Yeah, you know, God has a plan for you we love you."

Manfred decided to give up his old lifestyle and believed that hate and prejudice should be avoided and that God was the answer to everything:

Manfred: I'd say, around the first time I went into the mission. Those kinds of bondages of hate and prejudice, and all those things, I would say that was the point where I gave that up. I gave it to God, and He took it from me. I've never had to struggle with it, since then. To top it off, I have met my wife. I was raised very prejudiced, and when I went into the mission the first time, the faith-based program, I actually met my wife, and she was a black, Hispanic woman from Trenton, New Jersey. We were married for 17 years. She died last year.

The third invariant constituent or essential experience that followed the third theme was that one out of the 14 participants or 7% of the total sample population had a: Belief that being part of a gang was not moral thus allowed God to change him. The participant shared the following.

Jacob shared that he has always had the feeling that what he was doing was not right:

Jacob: Because, earlier in an earlier question you asked me about morality. There really was something gnawing at me on the inside that this just wasn't right, you know. Hurting people and doing these types of things just wasn't right.

— CHAPTER 7 —
Thematic Analysis 4

Theme 4. Had to change for their whole family and children to have the image and presence of a father.

The fourth main theme that emerged from the third research question which was the life-changing events that made former gang members leave their gang affiliations, it was known that most participants: Had to change for their whole family and children to have the image and presence of a father. This was deduced from eight invariant constituents (including the main theme) and can be seen in Table 5. The fourth theme of the former gang members sharing that the pivotal change for them was the realization that their family members, especially their children, needed a father received the highest number of responses with five out of the 14 total sample population or 36%.

Table 5

The Life-Changing Events that Made Former Gang Members Leave their Gang Affiliations

Invariant Constituents	# of occurrences	% of occurrences
Had to change for their whole family and children to have the image and presence of a father	5	36%
Realized one day that they hated what they have become as a person and decided to allow God to rescue them and make a change	2	14%
Loss of trust for the gang lifestyle	2	14%
Influenced by a great non-believer and gang member to have a better way of life with Jesus Christ as his Savior	1	7%
Influenced by the mother and family members when they converted as Christians to spread the Word of God and accept a new way of living	1	7%
Saw corruption at all levels in the group or gang and God intervened to save him	1	7%
Presence of constant fear as a member of a gang and decided to run away from the group	1	7%
No choice had to leave due to ceasefire but eventually believed that God rescued him	1	7%

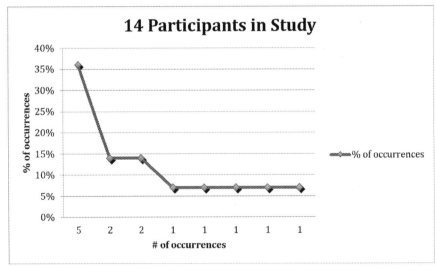

Figure 9. Graph representation of Table 5 – Theme 4.

Overall, the fourth theme that received the most responses from the participants was that they: Had to change for their whole family and children to have the image and presence of a father. The participants shared the following.

Martin stated that he had to decide to change for his family and children, as he did not want them to grow without a father. In addition, he also witnessed the lives of his friends and did not want to end up like them—in prison or dead:

> Martin: Because I had started a family, and my friends were going to prison or dying. I had a choice to make. Either I'm going to be in one of those two places ... my kids would grow up without a father or I've got to make a choice. I moved. I had to move from Florida to ... I don't live in the same place now, but within a few miles of where I used to live. It was myself and my best friend; we both left right around the same time. I moved to Tennessee and he moved to California. Figuratively speaking, we're the two that ended up doing the best.

Umberto shared that the main reason for him leaving the gang was the fact that he was a father already and that his wife started not to accept the kind of lifestyle that he had. One day, he witnessed someone giving the Gospel and allowed himself to be transformed:

> Umberto: I got married to this very beautiful cute girl, and we had a child in 1998, and it was just like we lost ... It's like being in a relationship where you are loved, but the person is not accepting what you are doing. She loves you or the person loves you for who you are, but that person is no longer going to go and hang out with you if you ... For me, it was a lot about skating, smoking marijuana, hanging out late hours and coming home, because I had a job. I would go to work at 6:00 in the morning, so I would come back from the clubs and stuff at 4:00 in the morning. My wife with our child was there, so yeah...
>
> After that it started to become harder and harder because you have a child and you want to be a dad. It's like, I want to give this kid everything, and then when you are constantly high and you are constantly hanging out in this environment that really doesn't produce anything, after a while people were falling off, people were getting arrested. A lot of my friends were getting involved in things that I just was afraid because I knew that it was going to affect my child and my life, but to be honest with you, the minute I left, that type of lifestyle was the minute I walked into this skateboard park inside the grounds of a church. It was a Tuesday night and somebody was giving the Gospel. Somebody was giving a Bible study, and he was using a skateboard to do that.

Gabriel stated that he left the gang because he wanted a new lifestyle and that he could not risk his family of being exposed to this kind of living anymore:

> Gabriel: Leaving the gang lifestyle…ehhh…being member of an organization, what we have tried to do is to redirect our lives by choosing a new lifestyle, the youngsters that are with us, share with us…and redirect them for good deeds.
>
> Well, seeing my mother suffer, watching my wife that was young visiting jail to see my daughter. You pray for all this, you don't want your children to be all that, right? You want the best for them. Not so, it was more my family and my love, because that has to do with God, right?

Peter stated that the essential change for him was that he did not want his mother to see him in prison anymore, considering how much she worked hard and suffered to raise them properly:

> Peter: Well what made me do this essential change was the fact that I was in prison, watching my mother working hard and I didn't want this for her. I don't want her to come and visit and I tell her that when I come out of jail not to worry that this will not happen again and that she won't suffer again for this kind of situation I went through, that it will be the last time.

Anibal admitted that he was forced by his family to change and transform and later on realized that what he was doing was not right and he indeed needed a transformation:

> Anibal: It wasn't by choice, this time, because my family found out how messed up I was. They had an intervention with me at my sister's house. They said, "You can either get help, or you can get out and never see us again." That hurts because my family is everything. I grew up in an Italian family, and my family was everything to me. My brother said, "You can never see your nephew again." My sister just had a baby niece, almost is a year now.
>
> I just felt horrible because I was doing drugs in the house where the baby was. I was filled with hate for myself. They're like, "Get help." I said, "Yes," but that night I still went and got high. I still did what I wanted to do. I left because I needed change, but I didn't want change.

The second invariant constituent or essential experience that followed the fourth theme was that two out of the 14 participants or 14% of the total sample population: Realized one day that they hated what they have become as a person and decided to allow God to rescue them and make a change. The participants shared the following.

Jacob stated that he saw himself one day in the mirror and hated what he had become as an individual. He always knew that God was there even in the darkest times and believed that God rescued him to change:

> Jacob: For me personally, if I look back throughout my life, and I had mentioned to you earlier that I had this, and I believe I was about 4 or 5 years old as far as I can remember, I had this experience with God. And I believed that God was real. And then throughout the different dark seasons of my life I knew he was still there. I knew that He was good and loving. I just had no idea how to have a relationship with Him. But the more I resisted Him, because I did resist Him, and the more I resisted God, the darker it became for me. Then the more despair and hopelessness that I experienced in my life. To the point that I wanted to die. I literally hated the man that I'd see in the mirror and lost hope, and felt death really closing in on me, almost literally. It was then that God came to my rescue and told me, in a matter of speaking; He told me that I needed to surrender to Him. The pivotal time was again nine years ago, when I knew I was lost if I didn't have Jesus in my life. Not just believe in Him, but have Him in my life and be surrendered to Him.

Jeremiah stated that he just allowed God to lead the change in his life and recognize how amazing Jesus is:

> Jeremiah: Yes, I would say the love for God. The love of Jesus and just the recognition of what Jesus did for me is truly amazing when you really understand the true Gospel and the sacrifice that was made for me as an individual and that God loves me (sighs). He sent His son for me, you know, to die on the cross, to love me. You know, when you start to wrap your mind around that in a personal way, it really compels you, to really worship Him. When you recognize and you really know who God is personally and how big He is, you know, He has made every star and the moon and the sun, you know, He's created everything. You know His plan is so perfect from beginning to the end, you want to be a part of that and when you trust in that and you live in that, then you just give your life for that and you start to understand it in a personal way, not just in a story but this is reality, it changes your life.

The third invariant constituent or essential experience that followed the fourth theme was that another two out of the 14 participants or 14% of the total sample population: Lost of trust for the gang lifestyle. The participants shared the following.

Elijah stated that the gang lifestyle was founded on trust and once he lost that trust he decided to leave his affiliations with them. When he needed them the most, it was the teachings through religion that saved him:

> Elijah: The gang lifestyle is founded on trust and when you come to the realization that that's not or it's not love because you can't trust someone that you don't love or that is not trustworthy. That is the key term I think for me, I trusted them, you trusted them with who you are, with your family, with your possessions and once that trust was ... I didn't see no different towards me as any other person then my importance in the gang to me seem I could be just another casualty another victim or another opportunity for the depravity or lack or morality to be used just another animal in the pen. So, I chose to get out of the pen.
>
> The pivotal change for me was when I really needed to have someone that I could go to and count on and get that truth and get the right answer and you have a solution and the only person that I found that in was that in the teachings of religion. I can't get that from any gang because gangs are just people and people are going to let you down because they're looking for their own self-interest. But when you look through a source that has no need of you and doesn't need to get nothing from you but ultimately is just trying to get something to you that really drove me to seeking that out because I wanted more of that freedom and the liberty to say I am no longer in bondage to needing to be on this gang /team. Now I'm on the path that leads me to seeking and finding what my purpose is in this life and along that way, along that journey I find these opportunities for me to give back to others and to do what we've all been created to do is to impact others along the way.

Manfred added that he lost the eagerness to be part of the lifestyle as he and his members wanted to face their responsibilities as adults and as individuals already:

> Manfred: I think, as we all grew up in age, we all just kind of had to start taking on responsibilities of life. There's only like, three of us left, out of the whole thing. We still stay in touch with each other. This is when I was 15 years old; I'm 45 now. We just grew up, and grew out of it, is really what it was. It didn't sustain. It was a group of us at that timeframe. It wasn't a legacy thing, where it kept on being passed down. Once we separated, it was just over with. We really just grew out of it with responsibilities of life, is really what it was.

The fourth invariant constituent or essential experience that followed the fourth theme was that one out of the 14 participants or 7% of the total sample population was: Influenced by a great non-believer and gang member to have a better way of life with Jesus Christ as his savior. The participant shared the following.

Adam stated that he decided to leave his gang affiliation when his best friend and childhood friend "Joey" changed his ways from being a big time loan shark to a firm believer of Jesus Christ. This transformation amazed Adam and allowed him to see the miracles and changes that may happen to him as well:

> Adam: When I came to Jesus Christ. Because I knew it was better way of life. A matter of fact the day I accepted Jesus Christ as my Lord and Savior I made a statement and I didn't know the power of it even when I made it. I'm realizing it more and more now it's guiding me a lot. Ten minutes after I accepted Jesus and was born again I made this statement, "I'm never going back."
>
> … Finally, I get frustrated I say, "Joey [best friend/ childhood friend], I … what … what's bigger?" I say, "You found God. You got Gotti." He says, "No, it's bigger than God." I say, "Joey, what's bigger than God?" He says, "I found Jesus Christ." I say, "I didn't know He was lost." He said to me and here was the clincher was with me … that was on the Friday, he says, "Come to my house." Now, his house is in Hollywood, Florida. It's a townhome in a complex of 16 townhomes. He built and owns them all and rent them out or sold them.
>
> I go to him and here's a man I know all my life. He's 30 years old. I'm 30 years old at that point … I'm 29. I hadn't seen him in six months. Number one, very good-looking man but you look at him you know you don't mess with Joey. I look at him, his whole countenance is different. That's Joey but that's not Joey.

The fifth invariant constituent or essential experience that followed the fourth theme was that one out of the 14 participants or 7% of the total sample population was: Influenced by the mother and family members when they converted as Christians to spread the Word of God and accept a new way of living. The participant shared the following.

Albert stated that he never wanted to leave the gang; however, through his mother and other siblings he was convinced to change when they converted as Christians and used the Bible to open many possibilities. The power of the Holy Spirit also guided him to make the big change:

> Albert: Actually, the desire is still there. I left the activity, but I am still there trying to work with the gang to bring them to Christ and to lead them to Christ. I left. It just came about when I had an encounter with Christ because, in reality, I was truly somewhat blind to truth and these things that God had been trying to speak to me through my mother. My mother became a Christian.

She started sharing the Word. Some of the brothers would come and share the Word of God. But I was blind for all this truth. I was blind for all these things. What happened, I almost died three times.

I spent 14 years in jail, in and out. The last time I was incarcerated, I was facing a double life sentence in prison. I was never going to get out. That's where it really hit, where I really reflected on my life. I would say: God used that moment for a moment of reflection in my life and to truly show me this is what your life is.

I left the gang. I will give testimony of Christ because myself, I couldn't go. I did it through the power of the Holy Spirit, the guidance of the Holy Spirit. I did it through the strength, the courage, the boldness that Jesus Christ did in my heart.

I truly, with all my heart, believe that ... I don't want to talk down on anybody or anyone that's doing any disservice to people. There are programs out there; there are people who have good teachings, who have good intentions of helping people. But the only way that we can receive a new heart is what the Bible says. That is through repentance and receiving of Christ that Christ can work in the hearts of men.

The sixth invariant constituent or essential experience that followed the fourth theme was that one out of the 14 participants or 7% of the total sample population: Saw corruption at all levels in the group or gang and God intervened to save him. The participant shared the following.

Roman stated that it was easy for him to leave his gang when the government changed and corruption from all levels emerged. This was also the time when God intervened and saved him as a person:

Roman: I did it for a very beautiful reason. I left it when there was an established government because I saw the corruption at all levels. And the only one who could have taken me away from there was God, nobody else.

Because when God manifests itself, I will explain it; there were many cases that when for instance soldiers that was with the regular regime, we captured and detained them, we executed them, but sometimes we couldn't do it. You know why? Because that man who was about to get shot, was a child of God. I do have a life testimony of this. I don't know if you have seen a movie called 'why do you cry?" a movie of China in war. The same thing happened with this girl, she was about to get executed and they couldn't. Because God intervened and used His hand.

The seventh invariant constituent or essential experience that followed the fourth theme was that one out of the 14 participants or 7% of the total sample population had the: Presence of constant fear as a member of a gang and decided to run away from the group. The participant shared the following.

Angel stated that he never wanted to be part of the gang in the first place as he was forced to join. He had constant fears as a member and one day decided to run and thankfully was never caught by the leaders of the gang:

> Angel: Man, I left it because it was so terrifying, every day seeing people killed and seeing people killed in a way that you never imagined; people being cut into pieces, people being, with machete, with a lot of things and it was something that I never really wanted to be a part of and I found myself in the midst of it and it's like every day I have dreams and every night I have dreams about someone that was killed, that was begging for his life, for our life and I feel like, man, I cannot take any of this anymore. So I got away. So I ran away with a friend of mine and I went to my general and asked him that I was going to go take some stuff from people so he allowed me to go and then my friend and I we left and we never returned.
>
> And they were looking for us, wanted to kill us but with God's blessing, they never found us. We never really came in contact with them.

The eighth and last invariant constituent or essential experience that followed the fourth theme was that one out of the 14 participants or 7% of the total sample population he had: No choice and had to leave due to Ceasefire but eventually believed that God rescued him. The participant shared the following.

Efraim stated that leaving the gang was not his choice but there was a Ceasefire during a Peace Agreement and he had to stop fighting. However, he believes that it was God's way of saving him and that there was a reason of doing so:

> Efraim: I don't think it was my choice but there was Ceasefire. I'd still be fighting today if there wasn't a Ceasefire. In fact I didn't know when I was going to be out. It wasn't you'll be here today maybe after a certain time you'll be out. You're out by death, you die, or there's just Ceasefire. So I'm out of the gang today. I could say maybe God … God had a reason. Now that I'm a Christian, I realized that but the only reason … because a couple of my brothers died. My brothers died in the wartime, so you leave the gang when you die or when the Ceasefire and it's like the Ceasefire now in the country for years so there is no war so people find different things to do.

Figure 10 that follows depicts a visual summary of the findings in which the four emerging themes are now four thematic categories.

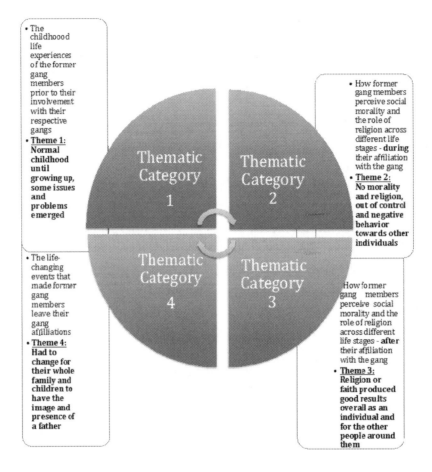

- The childhoood life experiences of the former gang members prior to their involvement with their respective gangs
- **Theme 1: Normal childhood until growing up, some issues and problems emerged**

- How former gang members perceive social morality and the role of religion across different life stages - **during their affiliation with the gang**
- **Theme 2: No morality and religion, out of control and negative behavior towards other individuals**

- The life-changing events that made former gang members leave their gang afﬁliations
- **Theme 4: Had to change for their whole family and children to have the image and presence of a father**

How former gang members perceive social morality and the role of religion across different life stages - **after their affiliation with the gang**
- **Theme 3: Religion or faith produced good results overall as an individual and for the other people around them**

Thematic Category 1

Thematic Category 2

Thematic Category 4

Thematic Category 3

Figure 10. Thematic categories summary – findings and emerging themes.

— CHAPTER 8 —
Findings and Emerging Themes

Based on the findings of the study, four themes emerged from the data. These themes fulfill the purpose of the study and address the research questions. These themes are:

a. Normal childhood until growing up, some issues and problems emerged,
b. No morality and religion, out of control and negative behavior towards other individuals,
c. Religion or faith produced good results overall as an individual and for the other people around them, and
d. Had to change for their whole family and children to have the image and presence of a father.

The first common theme among former gang members is "Normal childhood until growing up, some issues and problems emerged." This theme explains the experience of former gang members regarding factors that pushed them to become a member of a gang. Prior to being part of any gang, it was common for its members to have a normal childhood until they reached a stage where issues and problems emerged. The issues may take the form of family problems, social issues, or personal issues. These problems tend to become so complicated that individuals could not handle the extreme levels of stress it caused them, thus, pushing them to decide to live their lives as members of gangs.

The second theme that is common for former gang members is "No morality and religion, out of control and negative behavior towards other individuals." During their lives as gang members, they tended to live with disregard for any form of morality and religion, while focusing on exhibiting negative behavior toward others. These negative behaviors included aggression, violence, and rebellion, all of which have caused harm or hurt towards others around them. Such behavior is closely linked to the first theme of experiencing unmanageable problems and personal stress, which was the usual driver of their actions.

The third emergent theme common for former gang members is "Religion or faith produced good results overall as an individual and for the other people around them." More specifically, former gang members left their respective gangs without any intentions of going back to their old lives because religion and faith brought about renewed perspectives into their lives. Among these renewed perspectives is one with seeing no better life to live than one for Christ, who they see as their model of the right way of living. Also, renewed perspective in life, because of their religion, has brought about positive outlooks and positive changes within them and the people around them, including their respective families.

The fourth emergent theme for former gang members is "Had to change for their whole family and children to have the image and presence of a father." The pivotal and life-changing realization common for former gang members was their recognition that their family members, especially their children, needed a father in their lives. The realization that a life without a father at home to count on is not one which they want their children to grow up into, and thus, made them decide to leave the life of a gang member. This realization ultimately made them go back to being a good family man who lives the life based on faith and religion.

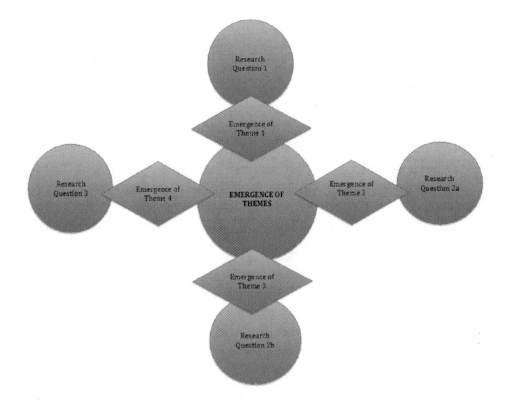

Figure 11. Model of emergence of themes.

— CHAPTER 9 —
The Grounded Theory HOPE©

Grounded on the data gathered and analysis for emerging themes, the present study developed the emerging theory called HOPE© which stands for *Holistic Outreach Program for Exit*. HOPE© postulated the role of faith and religion in the lives of former gang members, especially in their journey from being non-members of gangs to being former members of gangs. According to the findings of the present study, a theory on faith-based rehabilitation and gang membership has been developed, stating that, through a faith-based rehabilitation program, focusing on having a relationship with one's faith is an effective means of encouraging gang members to transform their lives and leave their gangs. Through such programs, gang members are encouraged to live a life free from aggression, violence, and behavior, which characterizes the life of a gangster (RQ2a), given the premise that they long for the betterment of their lives and the lives of the people around them.

In HOPE© theory, focusing on faith enlightens gang members to become aware of how the life of the faithful can bring back the meaning and fulfillment into a person's life, especially with knowing and having a personal relationship with God. Most gang members come from a normal and happy life as children, prior to the problems that propelled them into the gangster life (RQ1). From this emergent theme of having a normal and happy childhood to later having a gangster life, the realization that living a faith-based life, focused on their belief in God and the wonders that their God can do for them beyond what the gangster life has to offer, can make them see the possibility of bringing back normality, happiness, and fulfillment into the life of anyone, thus, aiding in their conversion from their gangster life back into the normal and happy lives they once used to experience as children (RQ2b). Moreover, having a relationship with their God made them realize the awful life they used to live as gangsters, making them more determined to cease their gang connections and affiliations (RQ2b). In addition, being a father makes this realization even more important because experiencing a normal and happy life once, makes them long for that same normal and happy life for their kids, thus, further preventing them from going back into their gangster life (RQ3). Finally, exposure to the faith and to religion gives gang members the hope and positivity that their lives can become better than how they were during their gangster days (RQ2b).

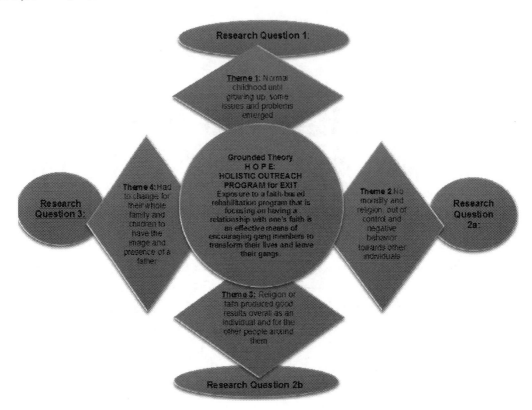

Figure 12. Model for Grounded Theory—HOPE©: Holistic Outreach Program for Exit.

Strengths and Limitations of the Study

One of the strengths of the study is that its data collection process was able to gather detailed information from former gang members to come up with emerging themes relevant to the research questions of the study. Also, the ability to show emerging themes that proved the important role of religion in promoting transformation in the lives of gang members is another strength of the study because it showed how faith and religion have been an effective aspect of rehabilitation that encouraged these former gang members to leave their gangster life and to have the courage to never go back.

An evident limitation of the study was that most of the respondents related to Christianity and Jesus as a living God, thus, being treated as a role model of how to live. This is a limitation because other religions do not regard Jesus as a God. Thus, the results may be limited to a focus on Christianity instead of all religions. Nevertheless, the study was still able to prove that focusing on one's faith in a rehabilitation program can encourage renewal and transformation in gang membership.

Implications for the field of Conflict Analysis and Resolution

Based on the themes that emerged from analysis, each theme corresponds to each of the research questions of the study. The first theme, which is "Normal childhood until growing up, some issues and problems emerged," addresses RQ1 that focuses on the experiences of former gang members prior to entering a gang. The second theme, which is "No morality and religion, out of control and negative behavior towards other individuals," addresses RQ2a which focuses on the role of religion and faith during membership in a gang. The third theme, which is "Religion or faith produced good results overall as an individual and for the other people around them," addresses RQ2b, which focuses on the role of religion and faith after gang involvement. The fourth theme, which is "Had to change for their whole family and children to have the image and presence of a father," addresses RQ3 that deals with the life changing event that made gang members quit their gangster life.

The resulting themes and HOPE© theory from the data gathering and analysis have several implications in the field of conflict analysis and resolution, especially when dealing with conflicts or issues related to gang membership. One of these implications is that there is a need to acknowledge potential inclusion of religion through its consideration or inclusion in programs for addressing negative behavior, specifically gang membership. Also, there is a need to focus on the past experiences when resolving problems or issues of human beings or society. Lastly, when dealing with conflicts related to negative behavior, religion must be considered as an important factor for change to positive behavior.

"But they that wait upon the LORD shall renew their strength: they shall mount up with wings as eagles; they shall run, and not be weary; and they shall walk, and not faint" – Isaiah 40:31

— CHAPTER 10 —

Proposal of MAPCID© Model

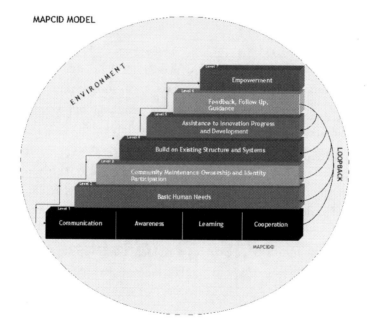

MAPCID MODEL

ENVIRONMENT

Level 7	Empowerment
Level 6	Feedback, Follow Up, Guidance
Level 5	Assistance to Innovation Progress and Development
Level 4	Build on Existing Structure and Systems
Level 3	Community Maintenance Ownership and Identity Participation
Level 2	Basic Human Needs

LOOPBACK

| Level 1 | Communication | Awareness | Learning | Cooperation |

MAPCID©

Figure 13. MAPCID©: Model for the Analysis of Potential Conflict in Development

(Smith, Michaud, Bertuna-Reynoso, & Struss. 2014).

On the basis of the MAPCID© model co-authored by the writer, it is accentuated by this research study the great importance in providing alternative options to prevent as well as rehabilitate individuals who have the potentials and/or engage in gang membership. Recommending MAPCID© as a concept for the background workings and foundation for the analysis of potential conflict in development is appropriate, as well as a research tool for a pilot study, and to initiate a faith-based rehabilitation program to deal with the social problem of gang membership in communities throughout the state of Florida to deter crime and recidivism.

According to Smith et al. (2014):

> over the last two decades, the development paradigm changed from top-down assistance provided by development organizations to local communities, to more collaborative processes between these parties (O'Brien, 2007). Scholars are now realizing there are differences in power, interests, values, decision-making ability, and expectations of outcomes between communities and development organizations (Barron, Diprose, & Woolcock, 2007; Oishi, 1995). This disparity led to the gradual marginalization or social exclusion of local poor people. With this paradigm shift, models for analyzing conflict in development projects are introducing additional measures of participation from the local level. (p.8)

Overall, this research study clearly showed no case study emerged of a faith-based gang exit program in Florida. Therefore, the MAPCID© model is recommended as an interpretive, instrumental tool to be used as a basis for future research in developing community faith-based rehabilitation programs in the state of Florida. The model's usefulness to the development of these programs would similarly follow the process as described here by Smith et al. (2014):

> scholars in the conflict resolution field are increasingly studying conflict in development projects. Generally, development is considered to be longer –term assistance that builds or develops a local community's economy and infrastructure. Practitioners are motivated to find new ways of effectively managing development interventions while minimizing conflict with local communities. (p. 7)
>
> A conflict practitioner can holistically analyze the context of the development project and recommend interventions to transform the conflict. Then, the poor community can become empowered by participation in the project. MAPCID© is designed for programming that is based on the local context or needs. (p. 9)

One possible approach for enhancement with emphasis on prevention, intervention, and support to deter future gang affiliation and membership is to introduce community faith-based interventions and assess them through the MAPCID© model. By going through each assessment level, MAPCID© is a very practical tool for this intervention process with its integrated loopback feature from tier to tier as shown in Figure 13.

The following is the consideration for analysis at each level of the MAPCID© model which allows the time and space for conflict to be reviewed and intercepted if need be by implementing intervening steps before moving to the next level of the development project, in this case faith-based rehabilitation program. These are the seven conflict assessment levels in the MAPCID© Model:

the analysis starts at the first level by reviewing the support structure, which facilitates the interaction between the parties. The support structure is a precondition for all parties to participate in the development initiative. The first level is achieved when effective communication occurs, there is a level of awareness for social change and a system for social learning and cooperation between parties is in place. In the second level, we evaluate the community's access to basic human needs to survive such as food, shelter, clothing, water, air and security. After these basic needs are met, the community does not have to worry about survival and can start thinking about development. The third level analysis is accomplished once the community is self-maintaining and employs cultural norms for participating in the project. After reaching this level, the community is socially and economically prepared for entering into development.

In levels four, five, and six we analyze how the development project is introduced and gradually integrated within the community. In the fourth level, the development organization steadily builds the project on the community's existing structure and systems. This level is completed once a suitable match is made between the community and the project. Level five analyzes the community's potential for developing innovative ideas and integrating them into the project. Then, the community takes full ownership and works side-by-side with the development organization to craft a path towards reaching the shared goal. In level six, we analyze how the development organization follows up and provides feedback on the activities planned by the community. Once the development organization has a system for providing this type of support, the community can be effectively guided towards reaching the shared goal.

In level seven, the integration of community and development organization is complete; the community has reached their goal and becomes empowered. The entire system of community/development organization/donor is often interrupted by outside forces. The system interacts with an outside environment, more specifically with the policy and institutional context. Institutions implementing national policies make available human, financial and legal resources that are felt at the local level. These measures can either stimulate or hinder the development path of the community. (Smith et al., 2014, pp. 10-11)

Reflections of the Author

I have several insights, reflections, and important aspects of the study that need to be highlighted. From the gathered data and analysis of the study it can be said that, indeed, faith was a positive contribution to the results of transformation with gang members. However, for most of the interviewees, it was not their religion per se that encouraged their transformation, but the relationship with their faith, and most of them related this to Christianity, Jesus as a living God that dwells in their hearts. In fact, the resonating affirmation I kept hearing over and over again through the interviews was that "if it was not for God, I do not know where I would be today; my life was destructive and with no purpose and now I know that I am a child of God." These statements highlight the importance of the role of the relationships that former gang members have with this heavenly father as it is what keeps them focused and prevents them from returning to their gangster lives once they have left. It was a very strong and emotionally defining affirmation for all of the respondents during their interviews.

The existing gap accentuated in the literature review was an important part of the entire study because it facilitated the focus of the research study on exploring the role that religion plays in gang membership removal. As stated in the literature review, while no case study emerged of a faith-based gang exit program in Florida, the review found that faith-based programs, especially if modeled on two of the most studied programs in California (Homeboy Industries and the Victory Outreach program), could be effective in expediting gang exit for gang members, thus, bridging the gap with a focus on faith, which was found to be an effective method for rehabilitation programs.

Concluding Comments and Thoughts

In summary, from the results of the study, faith was indeed a driver for transforming the lives of former gang members from being violent, aggressive, or rebellious, to being more positive and peaceful men living life based on their faith. It was evident throughout the interviews that former gang members, both young and old, all craved and lacked a father figure growing up, and those who had a father remember bad experiences or examples. This craving had them look outside in the world or out into the streets for a replacement of father and family. In line with this, it was also noted that more than once the words "to belong," "to be loved," and "to be accepted" were used by the interviewees who were willing to give up their lives for the gang. Indeed, this confirms what was mentioned in the literature review as the theme of belonging was noted as something that gang members long for.

Lastly, the absence in the state of Florida with regards to successful faith-based rehabilitation programs has been noted; hence, in line with the results of this research, consideration of these recommendations is crucial in order to make way and entertain the promotion and inclusion of such types of community betterment interventions throughout the state of Florida by offering faith-based rehabilitation programs. This lack of the much needed presence of successful and workable faith-based rehabilitation programs can only continue to contribute to the increase of gang membership and crime in the state of Florida.

I assert there is a gap in Conflict Resolution research concerning successful gang member rehabilitation. This book looks to fill that void by evaluating the social transformation and rehabilitation of former gang members via the use of faith-based approaches. By focusing on research concerning a faith-based approach to gang removal, the outcome allowed me to create the theory HOPE©. The culmination of the design of this theory was based on the application of a faith-based approach to rehabilitation of gang members.

Furthermore, I also co-authored MAPCID©, which allowed me to analyze conflict as an intrinsic part of development. It transcends a static view of conflict by capturing the dynamics between all parties involved during a development project. By following the model, one analyzes seven levels of conflict drivers, stimulates the continuous alignment of power, culture, and goals enabling timely participation of all parties in the development process. A faith-based gang exit program in Florida can be created, tested and assessed using MAPCID© as a pilot model.

Although there has been significant improvement in the nexus of Conflict Resolution and development, there is still a need for site-specific analytical tools that are able to capture the diversity, complexity, and dynamism of groups. This book offers the tools to address transformational "change".

"Blessed are the peacemakers, For they shall be called sons of God" – Matthew 5:9

References

Akers, R. L. (2010). Religion and crime. *The Criminologist, 35*(6), 1, 3-6.

Alleyne, E., & Wood, J. L. (2010). Gang involvement: Psychological and behavioral characteristics of gang members, peripheral youth and non-gang youth. *Aggressive Behavior, 36*(6), 423-436. doi:10.1002/ab.20360

Arthur, B. (2009). Managing gangs and STGs: Proactive approaches for safety and success. *Corrections Today, 71*(1), 8.

Attride-Stirling, J. (2001). Thematic networks: An analytic tool for qualitative research. *Qualitative Research, 1*(3), 385-405. doi:10.1177/146879410100100307

Baier, C. J., & Wright, B. R. E. (2001). "If you love me, keep my commandments": A meta-analysis of the effect of religion on crime. *Journal of Research in Crime and Delinquency, 38*(1) 3-21. doi:10.1177/0022427801038001001

Bangerter, O. (2010). Territorial gangs and their consequences for humanitarian players. *International Review of the Red Cross, 92*(878), 387-406. doi:10.1017/S1816383110000354

Barron, P., Diprose, R., & Woolcock, M. (2007, April). Local Conflict and development Projects in Indonesia: Part of the Problem or part of the Solution? (Working Paper No. 4212). doi:10.1596/1813-9450-4212

Bermudez, E. (2008, April 4). What's the latest gang symbol? Try the rosary. *National Catholic Reporter.* Retrieved from http://www.natcath.org/NCR_Online/archives2/2008b/040408/ss040408l.htm

Billitteri, T. J. (2010). Youth violence. *CQ Researcher, 20*(9), 193-216. Retrieved from http://sentencingproject.org/doc/news/inc_CQresearcher.pdf

Bogdan, R. C., & Biklen, S. K. (2006). *Qualitative research in education: An introduction to theory and methods* (5th ed.). Boston, MA: Allyn & Bacon.

Brenneman, R. E. (2009). *From homie to hermano: Conversion and gang exit in Central America* (Doctoral dissertation). Retrieved from ProQuest Dissertations and Theses database. (UMI No. 3406515)

Brenneman, R. E. (2010). *Pentecostal human rights activists? Religious motives in gang "rescue" programs in Central America.* Retrieved from http://www.american.edu/clals/upload/Brenneman_2010.pdf

Brown, S. C., Stevens, R. A., Jr., Troiano, P. F., & Schneider, M. K. (2002). Exploring complex phenomena: Grounded theory in student affairs research. *Journal of College Student Development, 43*(2), 1-11.

Bryant, A., & Charmaz, K. (Eds.). (2007). *The SAGE handbook of grounded theory.* Thousand Oaks, CA: Sage.

Buxant, C., & Saroglou, V. (2008). Joining and leaving a new religious movement: A study of ex-members' mental health. *Mental Health, Religion & Culture, 11*(3), 251-271. doi:10.1080/13674670701247528

Byassee, J. (2007). Gangs and God: How churches are reaching out. *The Christian Century, 124*(19), 20-28.

Calhoun, J. (2012, March). Partnering with the faith community to prevent youth and gang crime. *The California Cities Gang Prevention Network Bulletin, 25.* Retrieved from http://www.ccgpn.org/Publications/CCGPN%20Bulletin%2025.pdf, 1-8.

Creswell, J. W. (2005). *Educational research: Planning, conducting, and evaluating quantitative and qualitative research* (2nd ed.). Upper Saddle River, NJ: Merrill.

Creswell, J. W. (2009). *Research design: Qualitative, quantitative, and mixed methods approaches* (3rd ed.). Thousand Oaks, CA: Sage.

Cruz, N. (2006, March). New York gangsta's passion for God. *Challenge Newsline,* (59), 1-2.

Decker, S., & Pyrooz, D. (2011). Gangs, terrorism and radicalization. *Journal of Strategic Security, 4*(4), 151-166. doi:10.5038/1944-0472.4.4.7

Denzin, N. K., & Lincoln, Y. S. (2005). *The SAGE handbook of qualitative research* (3rd ed.). Thousand Oaks, CA: Sage.

Dnes, A. W., & Garoupa, N. (2010). Behavior, human capital and the formation of gangs. *Kyklos, 63*(4), 517-529. doi:10.1111/j.1467-6435.2010.00485.x

Duffin, C. (2011). Nurses successful at diverting gang members to youth support. *Nursing Standard, 26*(1), 7-13.

Eghighan, M., & Kirby, K. (2006). Girls in gangs: On the rise in America. *Corrections Today, 68*(2), 48-50. Retrieved from http://www.aca.org/fileupload/177/prasannak/Eghigian-Kirby-21.pdf

Erlandson, D. A., Harris, E. L., Skipper, B. L., & Allen, S. D. (1993). *Doing naturalistic inquiry: A guide to methods.* Newbury Park, CA: Sage.

Fleisher, M. (2009). Coping with macro-structural adversity: Chronic poverty, female youth gangs, and cultural resilience in the US African-American urban community. *Journal of Contingencies and Crisis Management, 17*(4), 274-285. doi:10.1111/j.1468-5973.2009.00589.x

Flick, U., Kvale, S., Angrosino, M. V., Barbour, R. S., Banks, M., Gibbs, G., & Rapley, T. (2007). *The Sage qualitative research kit.* London: Sage Publications.

Flores, E. (2010). *Faith and community: Recovering gang members in Los Angeles* (Doctoral dissertation). Retrieved from ProQuest Dissertations and Theses database. (UMI No. 3418254)

Ford, O. (2007). *"This is who I am": A phenomenological study of the lived experiences of black gay men with an undergraduate degree from a historically black college or university.* (Doctoral dissertation). Retrieved from ProQuest Dissertations and Theses database. (UMI No. 3292892)

Gardner, J. (2011). Keeping faith: Faith talk by and for incarcerated youth. *Urban Review, 43*(1), 22-42. doi:10.1007/s11256-009-0149-7

Glaser, B. G. (1965). The constant comparative method of qualitative analysis. *Social Problems, 12*(4), 436-445.

Glaser, B. G. (1978). *Theoretical sensitivity: Advances in the methodology of grounded theory.* Mill Valley, CA: Sociology Press.

Glaser, B. G. (1992). *Basics of grounded theory analysis: Emergence vs forcing.* Mill Valley, CA: Sociology Press.

Glaser, B. G., & Strauss, A. L. (1967). *The discovery of grounded theory: Strategies for qualitative research.* Chicago, IL: Aldine.

Glaser, B. G., & Strauss, A. L. (1999). *The discovery of grounded theory: Strategies for qualitative research.* New York, NY: Aldine de Gruyter.

Grekul, J., & LaBoucane-Benson, P. (2008). Aboriginal gangs and their (dis)placement: Contextualizing recruitment, membership, and status. *Canadian Journal of Criminology and Criminal Justice, 50*(1), 59-82. doi:10.3138/cjccj.50.1.59

Grobsmith, E. S. (1994). *Indians in prison: Incarcerated Native Americans in Nebraska.* Lincoln, NE: University of Nebraska Press.

Haynes, C. (2012, June 16). Rosaries, gangs and the battle over religious symbols in schools. *GazetteXtra.* Retrieved from http://gazettextra.com/news/2012/jun/16/rosaries-gangs-and-battle-over-religious-symbols-s/

Hiller, H. H., & DiLuzio, L. (2004). The interviewee and the research interview: Analyzing a neglected dimension in research. *Canadian Review of Sociology/Revue canadienne de sociologie, 41*(1), 1-26. doi:10.1111/j.1755-618X.2004.tb02167.x

Hoke, C. (2012, November 13). Jesus' barrio: Inmates as apostles. *The Christian Century.* Retrieved from http://www.christiancentury.org/article/2012-11/jesus-barrio

Hottman, C. (2009). How does violent crime cause individuals to join gangs? *Honors Projects.* Paper 18. Retrieved from http://digitalcommons.macalester.edu/cgi/viewcontent.cgi?article=1016&context=economics_honors_projects

Howell, J. C. (2010, December). Gang prevention: An overview of research and programs (NCJ No. 231116). *Juvenile Justice Bulletin,* 1-24. Retrieved from https://www.ncjrs.gov/pdffiles1/ojjdp/231116.pdf

Johnson, B. R. (1987a). Religiosity and institutional deviance: The impact of religious variables upon inmate adjustment. *Criminal Justice Review, 12*(1), 21-30. doi:10.1177/073401688701200104

Johnson, B. R. (1987b). Religious commitment within the corrections environment: An empirical assessment. In J. M. Day & W. S. Laufer (Eds.), *Crime, values, and religion* (pp. 193-209). Norwood, NJ: Ablex Publishing Corp.

Johnson, B. R. (2004). Religious programs and recidivism among former inmates in prison fellowship programs: A long-term follow-up study. *Justice Quarterly, 21*(2), 329-354. doi:10.1080/07418820400095831

Johnson, B. R. (2011, July). The religious antidote. *First Things: A Monthly Journal of Religion and Public Life,* (215), 23-25. Retrieved from http://www.firstthings.com/article/2011/07/the-religious-antidote

Jones, M. (2006). *Criminals of the Bible: Twenty-five case studies of biblical crimes and outlaws.* Grand Haven, MI: Faith Walk Publishing.

Jones, M., & Alony, I. (2011). Guiding the use of grounded theory in doctoral studies – An example from the Australian film industry. *International Journal of Doctoral Studies, 6,* 95-114.

Katz, C. M., & Fox, A. M. (2010). Risk and protective factors associated with gang-involved youth in Trinidad and Tobago. *Revista Panamericana de Salud Pública, 27*(3), 187-202.

Kelly, S. (2010). The psychological consequences to adolescents of exposure to gang violence in the community: An integrated review of the literature. *Journal of Child & Adolescent Psychiatric Nursing, 23*(2), 61-73. doi:10.1111/j.1744-6171.2010.00225.x

Kerley, K. R., Matthews, T. L., & Blanchard, T. C. (2005). Religiosity, religious participation, and negative prison behaviors. *Journal for Scientific Study of Religion, 44*(4), 443-457. doi:10.1111/j.1468-5906.2005.00296.x

King Ebstyne, P., & Furrow, J. L. (2004). Religion as a resource for positive youth development: Religion, social capital and moral outcomes. *Developmental Psychology, 40*(5), 703-713. doi:10.1037/0012-1649.40-.5.703

Koffman, S., Ray, A., Berg, S., Covington, L., Albarran, N. M., & Vasquez, M. (2009). Impact of a comprehensive whole child intervention and prevention program among youths at risk of gang involvement and other forms of delinquency. *Children & Schools, 31*(4), 239-245. Retrieved from http://jipp-la.org/pdf/Childrenandschools.pdf

Krohn, M. D., Ward, J. T., Thornberry, T. P., Lizotte, A. J., & Chu, R. (2011). The cascading effects of adolescent gang involvement across the life course. *Criminology, 49*(4), 991-1028. doi:10.1111/j.1745-9125.2011.00250.x

Landsberger, H. A. (1958). *Hawthorne revisited: Management and the worker: Its critics, and developments in human relations in industry.* Ithaca, NY: Cornell University.

Lincoln, Y. S., & Guba, E. G. (1985). *Naturalistic inquiry.* Beverly Hills, CA: Sage Publications.

Lin, A. C. (1998). Bridging positivist and interpretivist approaches to qualitative methods. *Policy Studies Journal, 26*(1), 162-180. doi:10.1111/j.1541-0072.1998.tb01931.x

Marshall, C., & Rossman, G. B. (1995). *Designing qualitative research* (2nd ed.). Thousand Oaks, CA: Sage.

Mehra, B. (2002). Bias in qualitative research: Voices from an online classroom. *The Qualitative Report, 7*(1). Retrieved from http://www.nova.edu/ssss/QR/ QR7-1/mehra.html.

Merriam, S. B. (2009). *Qualitative research: A guide to design and implementation* (2nd ed.). San Francisco, CA: John Wiley and Sons.

O'Brien, C. (2007). Integrated community development/conflict resolution strategies as 'peace building potential' in South Africa and Northern Ireland. *Community Development Journal, 42* (1), 114-130. doi:10.1093/cdj/bsi068.

Onwuegbuzie, A. J., & Leech, N. L. (2007). Validity and qualitative research: An oxymoron? *Quality and Quantity, 41*(2), 233-249. doi:10.1007/s11135-006-9000-3.

Oishi, M. (1995). Conflict resolution and development: A case study of domestic development and related conflicts in Malaysia. (Doctoral dissertation). Available from ProQuest Dissertations and Theses database. (UMI No. U072199)

Patton, M. Q. (2002). *Qualitative research and evaluation methods* (3rd ed.). Thousand Oaks, CA: Sage.

Polkinghorne, D. E. (2005). Language and meaning: Data collection in qualitative research. *Journal of Counseling Psychology, 52*(2), 137-145.

Richards, L. E. H. (1916). Elizabeth Fry: *The angel of the prisons*. New York: Appleton & Co.

Riley, W. (2006, April). Interpreting gang tattoos. *Corrections Today, 68*(2), 46-47, 51-53.

Rivera, L. G. (2010). Discipline and punish? Youth gangs' response to 'zero-tolerance' policies in Honduras. *Bulletin of Latin American Research, 29*(4), 492-504. doi:10.1111/j.1470-9856.2010.00415.x

Rubin, H. J., & Rubin, I. S. (1995). *Qualitative interviewing: The art of hearing data*. Thousand Oaks, CA: Sage.

Seidman, I. (2006). *Interviewing as qualitative research: A guide for researchers in education and the social sciences* (3rd ed.). New York, NY: Teachers College Press.

Simon, M. K., & Francis, J. B. (2001). *The dissertation and research cookbook from soup to nuts: A practical guide to help you start and complete your dissertation or research project* (3rd ed.). Dubuque, IA: Kendall/Hunt.

Smith G., Michaud, G. M., Bertuna-Reynoso, S., & Struss, P. K. (2014). MAPCID: A Model for the analysis of potential conflict in development. *Journal of Conflict Management, 2*(1), 7-32.

Smith, J. E. (1995). *Latino gang male youth and risk factors: Time preference, time perception, and locus of control* (Doctoral dissertation). Retrieved from ProQuest Dissertations and Theses database. (UMI No. 9616429)

Stern, P. N. (1994). Eroding grounded theory. In J. M. Morse (Ed.), *Critical issues in qualitative research methods* (pp. 212-223). London: Sage.

Strauss, A. L. (1987). *Qualitative analysis for social scientists.* New York: Cambridge University Press.

Strauss, A., & Corbin, J. (1990). *Basics of qualitative research: Grounded theory procedures and techniques.* New York, NY: Sage Publications.

Strauss, A. L., & Corbin, J. M. (1998). *Basics of qualitative research: Techniques and procedures for developing grounded theory.* Thousand Oaks, CA: Sage.

Sun, E. (2011). From gangs to God's child: Lecrae. *Christian Today.* Retrieved from http://www.christiantoday.com/article/from.gangs.to.gods.child.lecrae/28701.htm

Thomas, R. M. (2003). *Blending qualitative and quantitative research methods in theses and dissertations.* Thousand Oaks, CA: Corwin.

Thrasher, F. M. (1927). *The gang: A study of 1,313 gangs in Chicago.* Chicago, IL: University of Chicago Press.

Tortoroli, C. (2011). Gangs of New York are terrorists? The misapplication of the New York antiterrorism statute due to the lack of comprehensive gang legislation. *St. John's Law Review, 84*(1), 391-423.

Tyler, M. C. (2012). *Homeboy industries: Cycles of violence, religion and gangs in downtown Los Angeles* (Bachelor's thesis). Princeton University, Princeton, NJ.

Van Dyke, J. (2006, January/February). Worldview: Guatemala: Central American street gangs. *Youth Worker Journal,* 20-22. Retrieved from http://www2.crcna.org/site_uploads/uploads/crwm/Graphics/projects/WorldView-StreetGangs.pdf

White, R. (2009). Indigenous youth and gangs as family. *Youth Studies Australia, 28*(3), 47-58.

Willig, C. (2013). *Introducing qualitative research in psychology* (3rd ed.). New York, NY: McGraw-Hill Education.

Yearwood, D. L., & Hayes, R. A. (2000). *Perceptions of youth crime and youth gangs: A statewide systemic investigation.* Raleigh, NC: North Carolina Criminal Justice Analysis Center, Governor's Crime Commission.

Yin, R. K. (2009). *Case study research: Design and method* (4th ed.). Thousand Oaks, CA: Sage.

Zdun, S. (2008). Violence in street culture: Cross-cultural comparison of youth groups and criminal gangs. *New Directions for Youth Development, 2008*(119), 39-56. doi:10.1002/yd.272

About the Author

Dr. Susana J. Bertuna received her Ph.D. in Conflict Analysis and Resolution at Nova Southeastern University Graduate School of Humanities and Social Sciences, Fort Lauderdale, Florida. She also holds an M.B.A from St. John's University, and a B.S. in Economics from College of Staten Island of The City University of New York. Dr. Bertuna further possesses twenty plus years of experience as a successful business entrepreneur, specifically in the import/export market of home furnishing products from Europe, Latin America, and the Caribbean. The last culminating project within this field was in 2010, fulfilling the role as the FF&E Project Manager for the grand opening of the **W** Hotel in Miami, Florida.

Dr. Bertuna recreated her career and bridged it with her new found passion in Humanities and Social Sciences. While attending residence courses at Nova Southeastern University (NSU) she was associated with the Universidad Tecnologica Equinoccial in Quito, Ecuador teaching virtual classes in Spanish in the area of Conflict Analysis and Resolution. She was also an integral part from the inception and continues to support the Global Study Abroad program offered within the Department of Conflict Analysis and Resolution at NSU. Additionally, she was one of the founders of Christian Perspectives in Peacemaking, an initiative group launched in 2012. She co-authored an article presenting MAPCID©: Model for the Assessment of Potential Conflict in Development, published in April, 2014, in the *Journal of Conflict Management, Volume 2, Number 1*.

The vision of this book is a result of a seed planted in her heart back in 2010 during a study abroad program to Ecuador where the birth of the Hola Vida Project metamorphosed to the fruition of MAPCID©. Drawing from this inspiration she committed to be a voice for the voiceless. It was later rekindled and reinforced with two subsequent study abroad trips; one to Suriname in 2011, and a second one to Ecuador in 2012. Yet everything culminated during her own spiritual journey to Israel in 2012. She felt God's calling as she immersed her feet by the shore of the Sea of Galilee in Tabgha. There she stood captivated by a statue of Jesus and Peter near The Church of the Primacy of Saint Peter whose inscription read "Feed My Sheep". This has been tugging at her heart ever since.

Born in Buenos Aires, Argentina, from Italian immigrant parents, she is fluent in both Spanish and Italian. She has also lived in Italy, England, New York, Connecticut, New Jersey, and presently lives in Fort Lauderdale, Florida with her family. She loves writing, nature, travel, photography, decorating and cooking.

Raised in a developing country and educated in a developed country, having witnessed poverty and injustices during her extensive travels, Dr. Bertuna experienced an awakening to be part of the paradigm shift towards "change." She embraces and interprets "change" to be the contribution towards the transformation for a better and peaceful world. She refers herself as a hybrid of many learned behaviors, a colorful and flavorful combination of a human being. Her motto can be summarized thus: "as she gingerly plants seeds of hope every day walking through this journey called life, her passion continues". Her heart's desire is that collaborative works benefit all the voiceless: the poor, oppressed, marginalized, and especially the children in this world and future generations.

For more information contact Dr. Susana J. Bertuna at:
BERTUNA GROUP
www.bertunagroup.com
susanabertuna@gmail.com
www.linkedin.com/in/conflict2change

"The Fear of the Lord is the beginning of wisdom And the knowledge of the Holy One is understanding" – Proverbs 9:10

Printed in the United States
By Bookmasters